PREPPER'S SURVIVAL NAVIGATION

Find Your Way with Map and Compass as Well as Stars, Mountains, Rivers and Other Wilderness Signs

Walter Glen Martin

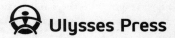

Published in the U.S. by
ULYSSES PRESS
P.O. Box 3440
Berkeley, CA 94703
www.ulyssespress.com

ISBN: 978-1-61243-672-2
Library of Congress Control Number 2016957544

Printed in the United States by United Graphics Inc.
10 9 8 7 6 5 4 3 2 1

Acquisitions editor: Casie Vogel
Managing editor: Claire Chun
Project editor: Shayna Keyles
Proofreader: Renee Rutledge
Index: Sayre Van Young
Layout: Jake Flaherty
Front cover and interior design: what!design @ whatweb.com
Cover artwork: © Sergei Drozd/shutterstock.com
Interior artwork: page 19 © BlueRingMedia/shutterstock.com;
  page 25 © satoja satuja/shutterstock.com; page 35 © Wellford
  Tiller/shutterstock.com

Distributed by Publishers Group West

To Jean,
my other North Star, for showing me the way.

CONTENTS

PREFACE

Preppers, survivalists, and many others know that preparing for disruptive possibilities gives peace of mind and can ensure safety and well-being. We each have our reasons to prepare. We talk about disasters, non-natural and natural; the economy, and a collapse; evacuations; bugging in, and bugging out. The list can be long, but always near the top is that possibility of not being home when disaster strikes. You may be unable to return home, or you may even be forced to leave your home. What would you do? Where would you go? Are you one of those that will bug out and just head for the mountains? Maybe you have that second home in the wilderness or a hunting buddy with a cabin in the woods. How will you find your way?

Putting all the doom and gloom aside for just a moment, I ask, are you an adventurer? Do you enjoy a weekend camping trip with the family? Maybe you love to fish and hunt those areas that other people seldom visit. Whatever the reason that finds you in the wilderness, whether it's a frightening scenario or a weekend outing with family, you should know how to get around in areas you're not familiar with and what you'll do when you find yourself lost.

Have you ever wondered what goes through the mind of another person or group of people who gets lost in the wilderness? If something like this has ever happened to you, then like me, you know that the worry can soon turn to fear, with panic being just a short step away. Never believe for a moment that you are immune to getting lost in an unfamiliar area. It happens all the time, even to the most experienced in outdoor activities. Whether it's a hunting excursion, a weekend camping trip, or a day picking huckleberries, circumstances can change due to an infinite number of reasons, and you'll be left wondering, "where am I, and how do I get home?"

When life is running smoothly and all seems well, we tend to become complacent. This is our nature. It always seems to be during these times of ease that disaster strikes, in one form or another. Disaster will almost certainly find us off guard. Are you prepared?

This book will provide you with a simple understanding of land navigation. You will find explanations of easy-to-use tools, methods, techniques, and ideas that will give you the ability to understand where you are, where you want to go, and how to find your way. You may say, "I have it covered. I have my cell phone and GPS device." A moment of thought will tell you that there are numerous reasons you may find yourself without use of electronic devices: damage, dead batteries, or you may simply not have these tools on hand when you need them.

It will require a little patience and practice to fully understand and confidently use many of the techniques and tools explained in this book. Keep this book with you for reference when you go on that family outing, spend a day at the park, or even explore in your own backyard. You can practice anywhere, at any time.

INTRODUCTION

As a young boy, I was raised on a dude ranch in a very secluded part of eastern Oregon, near the base of the Strawberry Mountain Wilderness Area. During the off-season, friends were as few and far between as the homes. Like any other kid growing up in the country, I had my chores around the house, like cleaning my room, milking cows, and tending to the animals. I also had school and homework assignments, which thrilled me less than mucking out the pigpens.

Fortunately, I also had spare time on weekends, holidays, and during summer vacations. During this time, you wouldn't find me at home, but hunting, fishing, or simply exploring somewhere in the wilderness nearby.

The J Bar L guest ranch was our home. My dad had purchased the dude ranch to ward off unwanted mischief, which my older brothers could not seem to avoid when we lived in the city. The ranch came with 12 small one- and two-room log cabins that could be rented out and were equipped much like motel rooms but included small fireplaces and stacks of wood. We had a game room with two pool tables, a Ping-Pong table, and an old-fashioned jukebox loaded with country music. The ranch had a lodge where family-style meals were prepared three times a day for all the guests. You ate what you were served, when it was served, or you waited until the next meal. It was a modest vacation spot for families who wanted to spend a week or two experiencing "cowboy" living.

There was also a large bunkhouse next to the swimming pool where groups of troubled kids from a special school in Portland would stay, giving them a chance to turn themselves around before entering juvenile custody or jail. The kids in these groups were given chores much like those my brothers and I had to do, like stocking the cabins with firewood, taking care of the horses, and keeping the bunkhouse clean. We were rewarded for our efforts with trail rides in the mountains and contests in the horse arena, including barrel racing and other activities. We also had access to swimming areas, hiking trails, ice-skating, and hayrides. There was a long list of things to do and adventures to take. It never occurred to me at the time that we were being taught how to work together and how to play safely and responsibly, all while discovering what it meant to be self-reliant and independent. We had a lot of fun.

I received my first compass when I was 12 years old. My dad always told me I had a case of "the itchy foot"—I always wanted to be on a journey. He also told me that once I learned how to use the compass, we would both find my countless trips into the woods much easier to deal with. During slow times, when we were waiting for new arrivals of kids or guests to the ranch, I practiced with my compass in the nearby wilderness. Taking a pencil, paper, and my compass with me on these trips, I began to make my own maps by walking off and noting distances and directions to caves, lakes, and other things that interested me. I never had a store-bought map back then, but I would have argued the maps I made were better.

As fall and winter arrived, hunters replaced the groups of kids and most of the vacationers. Summer fun was over, but what I considered the real excitement had just begun. Deer, elk, antelope, and bear were abundant, and as evidenced by the many head mounts that hung from the walls in our lodge, hunting these game animals was the main objective. The hunters came from all over the United Sates and on occasion from other countries. I remember one man in particular that came to us from England; he was not much of a hunter, but a great pool player.

While we prepared for these hunting trips, which we made by horseback and packhorses into the Strawberry Mountains, individual hunters stayed in the same cabins as our summer guests had, and larger groups of hunters stayed in the bunkhouse. This was no weekend for the novice, but a two-week-long adventure that would take place in extremely cold weather with some freezing rain, more snow, and a lot of tough terrain.

Our home base campsite had been established a few years before and had a large 12-person tent already in place. Since the site had already been stocked the previous year with nonperishable food, emergency medical supplies, a wood-burning stove for heat and cooking, extra blankets, and other supplies, our daylong pack trip to the campsite was less cumbersome. We had packed with us clothing, "fresh" food, hunting rifles, and other gear essential for our two-week stay. Among the essential items we each carried at all times were a small medical bag, a hunting knife, a small ration of food such as candy bars and jerky, a canteen of water, fire starters made from candle wax and sawdust, and a map and a compass.

We also made sure each member of the hunting party had a whistle, lighters for starting fires, and a strip of tire tread or vulcanized rubber for use as an emergency smoke signal.

When lit, the piece of tire tread put out a lot of heat and black smoke, which could be seen and smelled from several hundred yards away.

We had strict rules for our hunters to keep them as safe as possible and to make it easier to find anyone in case they became separated from the others or lost. The most important rule was that if anyone felt they may be lost or in any other danger, they should stay put and signal for help. Rules were followed, and we never had a problem that we could not easily deal with.

As hunting seasons came and went, I found that even at my young age, I was becoming the go-to person for planning the morning and evening hunts. Before dawn, we would gather and drink coffee near the cook stove, with the map of the area we were about to hunt laid out in front of us. I knew the best locations at which to position each hunter, where these positions were on the map, the trails we'd take to get there, and the distances and travel times to each stand.

I pointed out the most identifiable landmarks, their relationships to where we were, and their relationships to where a hunter would be placed. We identified on the map any obstacles that needed to be avoided and all potential hazards. We took inventory of each man's pack, making sure he had all the items needed to stay as safe and as comfortable as possible.

Growing up, the terms "prepping" and "land navigation" never occurred to me with any particular meaning. In those days, the term "prepper" did not even exist, and land navigation was just something I enjoyed learning and practicing. Now that I am older with the skills required for land navigation, I have found that to be successful in land navigation, you must also be a prepper, and to be a prepper, you should have skills in land navigation. As Forrest Gump might say, "Prepping and land navigation is like peas and carrots."

The Importance of Being Prepared

Prepping is a lifestyle now embraced by millions of people across the globe, and especially in today's world, more people should embrace the prepping mindset. Along with the natural and non-natural disasters that happen all too often, an endless number of potential threats can affect our daily lives. A volatile economy, cyber warfare, terrorism, weapons of mass destruction, interstate conflicts, and infectious diseases are just a few of the top threats facing the world,[1] as listed in an article from *USA Today*.

From the nine-month period between January 1, 2016, and September 30, 2016, the Federal Emergency Management Agency (FEMA) reported no less than 71 different disaster declarations in 34 different states.[2] The disasters reported range from severe storms, tornadoes, and flooding to landslides, mudslides, contaminated water, and fire. According to a report by the National Centers for Environmental Information (NCEI), eight events between January 2016 and July 2016 each caused over $1 billion in losses across the United States.[3] These eight events resulted in the deaths of 30 people, caused significant economic repercussions, and affected thousands of families.

Disasters are not limited to those that affect hundreds or thousands of people in a single event. Disasters are quite common on a more individual level and happen all too often. A personal disaster could include job loss, vehicle breakdown, death of a loved one, an accidental house fire, or any other incident that leaves a person incapable of supporting his or her family.

1 Kim Hjelmgaard, "The Biggest, Baddest Threats We Face over the Next 10 Years," *USA Today*, Jan. 15, 2015, http://www.usatoday.com/story/news/world/2015/01/15/global-risks-report-2015-world-economic-forum/21794757.

2 "Disaster Declarations for 2016," FEMA, Accessed Jan. 2017, https://www.fema.gov/disasters/grid/year/2016.

3 "Billion-Dollar Weather and Climate Disasters: Overview," National Centers for Environmental Information, Accessed Jan. 2017, https://www.ncdc.noaa.gov/billions.

Who you are, where you live, and the life you lead determines the list of potential problems that can set you back or turn your world upside down. A family living in sunny central California may not be concerned about a winter blizzard; instead, they prepare for a potential earthquake that could level their home and close down their city. The family living in rural Kansas may not be worried about a riot in New York City as they stock up their storm shelter for the possibility of a direct hit by the next tornado.

Why Land Navigation?

While all preppers try to prepare for the possibility of a life-changing event or threat, including many of those listed earlier, few consider the very real possibility that such an event or threat could thrust them into surroundings they may not be familiar with. Even if you have that bug out bag, where will you go? If you have a bug out location, how will you get there if conventional means of transportation are not available? Roads may be closed and alternate routes may be unavailable. Do you have the knowledge to get from point A to point B, or will you get lost when the unthinkable happens? If you're lucky enough to make it to your destination, are you familiar with the area? How will you move around to procure food and water without getting lost once you arrive?

Most people have never had the experience of being lost, but the likelihood of getting lost increases for those that spend a great deal of time engaging in outdoor activities, such as camping, hiking, or backpacking. The ones most likely to find themselves lost are the ones with the least amount of experience in land navigation.

"After 2 days, chances of finding lost people alive are slim."
—Oregon Health and Science University

A study conducted by Oregon Health and Science University created a model to determine "when a search and rescue (SAR) mission could be terminated without abandoning potential survivors. The model found time to be the most important variable in determining whether a person will be found alive. Ninety-nine percent of people found alive were found within the first 51 hours after being reported missing." The study looked at the 4,244 SAR missions conducted in Oregon between 1997 and 2003.[4]

There are two very important points to take away from this study. The first is that in only 6 years, there were 4,244 search and rescue missions in the state of Oregon alone. The second thing to note is that once lost, the odds of being found after 51 hours are only 1 percent.

The importance of being able to find your way through the landscape is not limited to disaster scenarios. The basics are relatively simple to learn; understanding them will give you an opportunity to expand on other activities you and your family may enjoy. If you're a person who enjoys the outdoors, you'll find yourself unknowingly using the skills you learn in this book. You'll go places you wouldn't have gone before and begin exploring areas that you may have avoided in the past for fear of becoming lost. Opportunities for new, original family outings and vacation spots will open up. Land navigation is also a fun skill that children love to learn, and it will give you peace of mind to know they have that skill when they venture out into the wilderness.

---

4 "OSHU Researchers Find Time Is Best Predictor of Survival in Search and Rescue Missions," Oregon Health and Science University, July 17, 2007, Accessed Jan. 2017, https://news.ohsu.edu/2007/07/17/ohsu-researchers-find-time-is-best-predictor-of-survival-in-search-and-rescue-missions.

FINDING NORTH WITHOUT A COMPASS

Knowing the four cardinal directions is essential to reading a map and learning navigation. The sun, and its relationship to the earth, is a unique tool that can help you determine direction. When facing north, the sun will always rise on your right (east) and set on your left (west). Also, remember that the sun will be at its highest point at midday. At midday in the Northern Hemisphere, the sun will indicate due south and will cast no appreciable shadow. If you're located in the Southern Hemisphere, this same midday sun will mark due north.

Finding north in bad weather, or on cloudy nights when the stars cannot be seen, is not often possible without the aid of a compass. Under these circumstances, the best option could be to find suitable shelter and wait for help or for the weather to change. If you're equipped with a compass, these conditions may not be a problem. Without a compass, these simple techniques may still help.

Using the Sun to Find North

Using the sun for navigation may be the oldest method known by humankind. However, if I were to ask you the simplest of questions about the sun—"in what direction will the sun rise?"—the answer I would expect to hear would be east. If you answered east, you would be right. But on only two days of the year, during the equinoxes, would you be *exactly* right.

An equinox occurs every six months, or twice a year, first around March 20, and again near September 23. During an equinox, day and night last for approximately the same duration. On these two days, the sun rises due east and sets due west. All other days of the year, the sun rises somewhere south or north of due east.

As the earth rotates, giving us day and night, it also travels around the sun, giving us our seasons. The reason for the change in climate during different seasons and the length of days and nights lies in the tilt of the earth. At the solstices, which also happen every six months, the earth's tilt is at its most extreme angle. In June at the summer solstice, the North Pole is tilted toward the sun. This tilt toward the sun gives us our longest day, with the sun rising farthest north of east. Six months later on the winter solstice, the North Pole is tilted farthest away from the sun. With the North Pole tilting away from the sun and the sun rising at its farthest south from due east, we experience shorter days. During sunset, the tilt of the earth remains the same, so if you have a northeast sunrise, you'll have a northwest sunset.

Your latitude and the time of year will determine the exact location of sunrise and sunset relative to where you're standing. The farther north or south from the Equator you are, and the closer you are to one of the solstices, the farther the sun will rise or fall from due east or due west. When in the

Arctic Circle in June, the sun rises so far north of east that it actually never sets.

Say you're camping during the month of an equinox and you take a walk toward sunrise. At the end of the day, you turn around and head back toward the sunset. There's a good chance you'll find your starting point. However, if you tried taking this same walk in midsummer or midwinter, you would never come across your starting point because the sun does not rise due east and set due west. In midsummer, the sun sets in the northwest sky, so to return to your starting point, you would need to follow a northeasterly course on your return trip.

Keep it simple. Think about the season and consider the earth's tilt. No matter where you are in the world, this will give you the answer to which side of east and west the sun will rise and set on that day.

Without hundreds of hours of practice, traveling by sun alone is good for short distances at best. But if you're traveling during, or very close to, an equinox, longer distances can be navigated with greater accuracy and less chance of error.

The Shadow Tip

No matter where you are in the world, you can use shadows to find your bearing (directional orientation). The shortest shadow cast each day will give you a perfect north-south line; this happens at midday. You can create this shadow with a stick placed vertically in the ground.

The shadow-tip method for finding north is the most commonly used. For the maximum degree of accuracy, it should be practiced as close to the noon hour as possible. It requires only a stick; a clear, level spot on the ground; and enough sun to cast a shadow. The taller the stick and the narrower the tip, the more accurate the reading will be.

1. As close to the noon hour as possible, place a stick in the ground vertically so it casts a shadow.

2. Mark the tip of the shadow with a rock or a scratch in the dirt, making sure you can identify the mark later.

3. Wait 15 to 20 minutes, and mark the new position of the shadow's tip.

4. Now, facing away from the stick, place your left foot on the first mark (west) and your right foot on the second mark (east). You'll be facing relatively north, with south behind you.

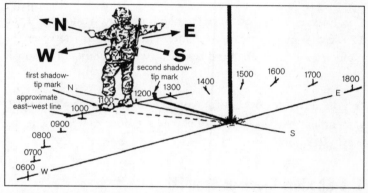

Telling time with the shadow tip

For better accuracy, place your stick in the ground at least half an hour before midday, and with a string or another object, measure the length of the stick's shadow. Then mark the shadow's tip. As the sun reaches the midday point, the shadow will shorten, and after midday, the shadow will begin to lengthen again. As the shadow lengthens, take periodic measurements with the string until the length of the shadow is the same as it was at your first measurement. Mark the shadow's tip. The midpoint between the first shadow-tip mark and the second shadow-tip mark will be a perfect north-south line. As before, you can place your left foot on the first mark (west) and your right foot on the last mark (east), and you will be facing true north.

The Analog Watch

The analog watch method can also be used to find north. To do this, place the watch on a level surface or hold the watch horizontally, and then point the hour hand toward the sun. Bisect the angle between the hour hand and the 12 o'clock mark to give you the north–south line.

If your watch is set for daylight savings time, you must set your watch back one hour from the time shown.

If you were in the Southern Hemisphere, you would point the 12 o'clock mark toward the sun. The midpoint between 12 o'clock and the hour hand would give you your north-south line.

If you have doubts as to which end of the line is north, remember that the sun is in the east before noon and in the west after noon.

The Shadow Clock or Sundial

Once you have found north, you can estimate the time of day using the shadow stick. To do this, place your stick vertically in the center of an imaginary line between the west shadow-tip mark and the east shadow-tip mark. The shadow created by the stick will now become the hour hand, with the west shadow-tip mark representing 0600 hours, or 6:00 a.m., and the east mark representing 1800 hours, or 6:00 p.m. A north-south shadow line represents the noon hour.

In the Southern Hemisphere, the sun still rises in the east and sets in the west, but north of the equator. This will effectively create a clock that runs counterclockwise.

The shadow clock isn't like a conventional timepiece with six equal hours before and after midday. Depending on location and the date, days may be shorter or longer, giving unequal hours before and after the noon hour. With a shadow clock, sunrise will be at approximately six in the morning and sunset at around six in the evening, with 12 unequal hours between. This is because there are generally no recognizable shadows cast before six in the morning or after six in the evening. When a typical timepiece is not available, the shadow clock will provide a satisfactory way of telling time. The shadow clock is not suitable in polar regions.

Creating a sundial at home is a great way to involve the kids in learning. Also, you can obtain great accuracy by using a watch to set up your sundial. The process is the same as creating a shadow clock, with a few exceptions. First, you can now make a base with any number of materials, from cardboard to plywood to concrete, depending on how permanent or elaborate you want it to be. Keep in mind that you must attach a stick, dowel, or other suitable item in the center of your base to cast the shadow. With a watch set to the correct time, start at 6 o'clock in the morning and make a mark or place a stone at the shadow's tip. Make a new mark at the shadow's tip each following hour, with the last mark made at 6 o'clock in the evening.

Navigating at Night

"He pointed out to him the bearings of the coast, explained to him the variations of the compass, and taught him to read in that vast book opened over our heads which they call heaven, and where God writes in azure with letters of diamonds."

—Alexandre Dumas, *The Count of Monte Cristo*

As with bad weather, the inexperienced should avoid traveling at night whenever possible. Even experienced outdoor enthusiasts will avoid traveling at night unless it's absolutely necessary and they are sure of the terrain. Without the ability to clearly see obstacles and potential threats, nighttime travel is slow and can become very dangerous.

To navigate at night without a compass or other instruments for guidance, you must have some basic knowledge of stars and star formations. When looking up into the night sky, you may think it a daunting task to figure out how to find north. The night sky is a maze of stars in constant motion. However, with just a little practice and observation, you'll soon find how simple it really is. Like the sun can help you find north, the stars can also help you find your way. On any clear night, over 5,000 stars may be visible to the eye, but only a handful of stars and even fewer constellations are needed to find north.

Polaris, the North Star

We know that the night sky always changes with the seasons or time of year. Even during a single night, you can see how the earth's rotation and its travel around the sun appear to make the stars move across the sky. There is one star, however, that seemingly remains stationary all night, every night throughout the year. Polaris, better known as the North Star, always remains in its place in the sky as all the other stars and constellations revolve around it.

The North Star isn't the brightest star in the sky, but it's the most important due to its location. The further north you are, the higher the star will appear in the sky. In the Northern Hemisphere, it's the most common point of reference in navigation.

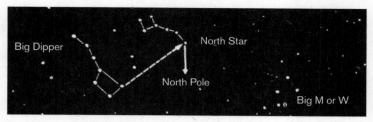

Finding the North Star using the Big Dipper

To find the North Star, you must first locate Ursa Minor, better known as the Little Dipper. The North Star is the last star in the handle of the Little Dipper constellation. If you have trouble locating the Little Dipper, find the Big Dipper (Ursa Major). "Spring up and fall down" is an old saying to help people find the Big Dipper. Always located in the northern sky, the Big Dipper is highest in the night sky during spring and summer months. During autumn and winter nights, the Big Dipper lies closer to the horizon. When searching for the Big Dipper in autumn or winter, be careful that your view is not being obstructed by trees, mountains, or other obstacles that may be hiding it.

Because of the earth's rotation, the stars and constellations appear to revolve around the North Star. As the seasons change, so does the orientation and location of the Big Dipper. To make it easier to locate the Big Dipper, remember these simple rules:

- In the fall, the Big Dipper appears most like its namesake, with its cup facing up. Because it's also nearer the horizon, it can be imagined as lying on a table catching falling leaves.

- During the winter season, the handle of the Big Dipper can be thought of as an icicle hanging from a bowl.

- In spring, think of spring showers. The Big Dipper will be higher in the night sky, upside down and spilling water from its cup.

- In summer, when the weather is hotter, you'll find the bowl of the Big Dipper reaching down to gather a cup of water.

The two outer stars in the Big Dipper's cup will point to the North Star. From the cup's outer bottom star through the upper star of the cup, form a straight line five times the distance between these two stars to reach the North Star; you can find an example of this on the image on page 17. Once you have found the North Star, draw an imaginary line straight down to the earth and the North Pole. This works regardless of the time of year and the Big Dipper's orientation.

Polaris is too high in the sky to be of any use if your latitude is above the 70th parallel. Also, for those living south of the Equator, Polaris isn't visible at all, and other stars or constellations are necessary for finding north. In the Southern Hemisphere, no single star is bright enough to give us directions, so for Southern Hemisphere navigation, use the constellation Crux, also known as the Southern Cross. The

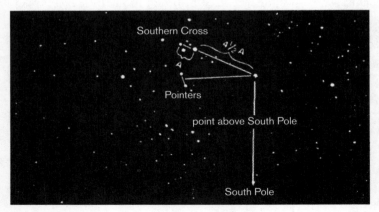

Southern Cross

Southern Cross is made of five stars, with four of the brightest taking the shape of a leaning cross. The pointer stars are the two that make up either end of the long axis of the cross. To find south, imagine a line from the pointer stars to the horizon.

The Moon

The crescent moon can be used as a way to find direction at night. Because the moon produces no light of its own, we rely on the light of the sun reflecting off its surface. A compass would be a much more accurate way of finding direction, but if you're without a compass, this relationship between the sun and the moon works to give an approximate direction.

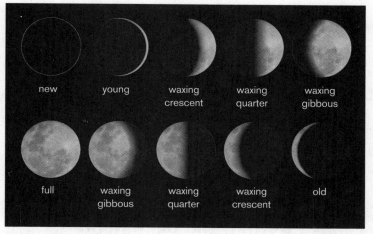

Phases of the moon

The moon rises and falls, like the sun does, in a general east-to-west direction across the night sky. Because the sun and the moon orbit the earth at different speeds, the light reflected off the moon changes shape throughout the moon's 28-day orbit. As the moon orbits the earth, the area of light reflected will either increase (wax) from the right side until the moon is full and fully illuminated; or, the reflection will shrink (wane) toward the left, creating a crescent shape and eventually a new moon.

When using the moon for navigational purposes, a crescent moon is the fastest and simplest way to find direction. Imagine a straight line that starts from the upper tip of the crescent, hits the lower tip, and then continues until it reaches the horizon. The point where this line meets the horizon indicates a general southerly direction. In the Southern Hemisphere, you can use this same technique to indicate north. It's important to remember that while this method is less than accurate, it becomes less reliable when the moon is closer to the horizon. Use this method only when the moon is highest in the sky, just after sunset.

There is a much more accurate way of finding north using the moon. This method works much like the shadow-tip method for solar navigation, explained on page 12. However, it requires you get little to no sleep. To use the moon's shadow, place a stick or another similar object in the ground. When the moon is bright enough to cast a shadow, periodically mark the shadow's tip. During the night, a curved line formed by the marks will become clear. The shortest distance between the stick and these marks is your north-south line.

Finding North Using the Natural Environment

Moss. Contrary to popular belief, you cannot always find north by the growth of moss on a tree because moss can grow all the way around some trees. However, growth will generally be lusher on the side of the tree that is facing north if you're in the Northern Hemisphere and on the southern side of the tree if you're in the Southern Hemisphere. While this may be convenient for a sense of direction, it provides little accuracy for finding true north. However, there are things you can look for to increase reliability.

Moss will grow more abundantly where moisture is the heaviest. Ask yourself: Why is the moisture concentrated here? If the moss is close to the ground, it may be drawing moisture from ground evaporation rather than the tree or rock it's attached to. It's usually a good idea to avoid consideration of moss within 2 feet of the ground. The less vertical a surface or the courser the surface is, as in heavy tree bark, the slower water runoff will be, and moss will thrive in this moisture.

Look at several trees or other near-vertical, off-the-ground surfaces. The smoother the surface, the better. The most likely reason you'll find moss in those locations is that it is in the shade, still collecting moisture while the sun is drying things out.

Trees. Studying the growth of trees can give you another source of direction. In the Northern Hemisphere, the south side of the tree receives the most sun and is generally heavier and lusher. Another clue is in the branches. On the northern side of a tree, the branches will tend to grow more vertically than on the southern side. This is due to the northern branches reaching higher to obtain the sun's light, while branches on the southern side already receive plenty of light and tend to grow horizontally. You may also notice that the growth rings in the stumps of trees will be spaced farther apart on the side facing south. Forested or woodland areas where trees compete for sunlight may make it confusing; however, you can use the growth patterns of trees standing alone to help guide you.

Landscape. In the Northern Hemisphere, you may find north by observing hills or mountains. Because the sun is due south at midday, north-facing slopes stay cooler and retain more moisture. You're likely to see more snowfall on the northern slopes in winter and more patches of snow as the season turns to spring and then summer.

Animals. Animals provide us with little assistance in finding true north. However, many animals, like geese, are migratory, and we know through research that they find their direction using the earth's magnetic field. Other studies have shown herds of cattle will generally face a north-south direction while grazing.[5] And still another study shows that dogs will generally face a north–south direction while pooping.[6]

5 "Cows Tend to Face North-South," *Scientific American,* August 26, 2008, Accessed Jan. 2017, https://www.scientificamerican.com/podcast/episode/FB9B3CC3-E299-DCDD-838FD5 34037D00CB.

6 "Dogs Poop in Alignment with Earth's Magnetic Field, Study Finds," *PBS Newshour,* January 3, 2014, Accessed Jan. 2017, http://www.pbs.org/newshour/rundown/dogs-poop-in-alignment-with-earths-magnetic-field-study-finds.

THE TOPOGRAPHICAL MAP

Whether you're going to the country to visit friends, taking a weekend camping trip to your favorite spot, or getting ready to bug out, get a map of the area you'll be visiting, even if you already know the surroundings. Study the map and compare it with what you already know; this is great practice for reading and understanding maps of unfamiliar places. You'll probably see that things look a little different on the map. Things may appear larger, or in a different location or orientation than you thought they would be. Along with showing you the cardinal directions, a map will also show you the way to adventure, sites you may not have otherwise seen, and maybe even places no one has ever been. To guide you through an adventure out into the unknown, to survive on your own, and to thrive in the wilderness, there is no substitute for the topographical map.

Any seasoned prepper, survivalist, or outdoor enthusiast will tell you that the topographical map could be the most important tool you will ever own. Unlike a regular map, a topographical map allows you to see a landscape in three dimensions. Information about land contours and elevation sets these maps apart from all other maps. They provide a view from above the earth to the landscape below, giving a detailed representation of an area's natural and non-natural features. The locations, elevations, and distances of rivers, lakes, mountains, and valleys can all be seen. Not only can your map give you landmarks and distances, it will also show you potential obstacles or threats, both natural or non-natural, thus saving you time by allowing you to determine safe alternate routes.

Topography maps are essential to navigation, with a history of more than 5,000 years. The simplest form, which we have all used as a child, is made with a stick and a patch of dirt, or pencil and paper. Modern maps use today's technologies, like satellites and special surveying techniques, to give us very high precision and consistency. While we all have the ability to draw with a stick in the dirt, very few of us have the ability to read and fully understand a modern topographical map.

Also called topo maps, topographical maps are available in different scales and can be found on the Internet, at libraries, at bookstores, or at your local, state, city, or county offices. The most common topo map, which we will use in the chapters ahead, is the 24K topo. The 24K topo map shows detail on a scale of 1:24,000, where 1 inch on the map is equal to 24,000 inches, or 2,000 feet, on the ground.

As a rule, all modern maps are oriented so that when looking at the map, north is at the top, south is at the bottom, the left edge of the map is west, and the right is east. It's always a good idea for you to be facing north whenever looking at your map.

Symbols and Features

A map can tell us a number of things, and many of these things are described with symbols. Each symbol is unique and represents a different feature on the map. A list of these different symbols and their meanings is usually found below or beside the map. These symbols often include natural or non-natural items or points of interest to help the reader navigate the area. Common symbols include primary and secondary roads; paved, gravel, and dirt roads; and gates and barriers. Other symbols used on any given map may be found within the map itself and depend greatly on what features are unique to that area. The most common symbols, found on many topographical maps, are contour lines, which provide the reader with elevations and contours of the terrain. Ridges, valleys, mountains, and their locations will all be shown in detail.

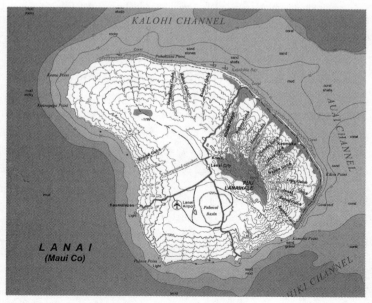

Example of a topographical map

Contour lines. Most experienced adventurers who use topographical maps would agree that the most important symbols on a map are the contour lines. Dominating the map, these wavy lines represent elevation. The elevation is the same at any point along each line. The darker lines are referred to as index lines; you'll typically see the elevation printed on these lines. The four lighter lines between each index line are known as intermediate contour lines. You may not notice elevations written on the intermediate lines, but the elevations are easily calculated by taking the difference between two parallel index lines, dividing by five, and then adding the resulting number to each ascending intermediate counter line. For example, if an index line is marked at 3,200 feet and the index line below it is marked at 3,000 feet, you can calculate the intervals between each intermediate line as

$$3,200 \text{ feet} - 3,000 \text{ feet} = 200$$

$$200 \text{ feet} \div 5 = 40 \text{ feet}$$

The first intermediate contour line below the 3,200-foot index line would thus be 3,160 feet.

The distance between contour lines represents the slope, or steepness, of elevation. Any two parallel index lines or intermediate lines spaced very close together will represent a steeper slope. Lines that are extremely close or on top of each other represent a fall hazard or cliff. The farther apart the lines are, the less slope there will be.

Ridges and valleys. Ridges and valleys are also important features to recognize. The contour lines of both have the appearance of "V" shapes and can easily be confused with one another. The "V" will always point downhill for ridges and uphill for valleys. This can easily be seen on a map where water is flowing down a creek. You'll see the water flowing against the "V."

Unique features. Other features of importance may not be listed as symbols on the legend but may be shown within the map. Features like rivers, streams, lakes, forests, deserts, and rock formations, as well as non-natural objects like bridges, tunnels, power lines, water towers, fences, and buildings, may be found on a map. See the image on page 59 for some examples.

Scale

It's impossible to effectively plan a trip across country, or even across a stretch of wilderness, without knowing how far you're traveling. Without a scale to measure distance, even your best guess may have you in the darkness long before you reach your destination. Usually found at the bottom of any map is a scale that allows the user to convert the distance between two points on the map to the distance between two points on the ground.

Topographical maps will generally have a numerical scale and a bar scale at the bottom of the map. The numerical scale, also called the representative fraction (RF) scale, is usually written as a fraction. As mentioned earlier, the 24k topo is at a scale of 1/24,000. On this map, 1 inch equals 24,000 inches, or 2,000 feet. Whichever unit is used on the map would be multiplied by 24,000 on the ground. For example, $1\frac{1}{2}$ inches would be read like this:

(1 inch = 2,000 feet) + (½ inch = 1,000 feet) = 3,000 feet.

For measuring distance, we are most interested in the graphic, or bar, scale. Maps will usually show three or four graphic scales. The four most common units of measurement represented on these scales are feet, miles, meters, and kilometers. Each scale is divided into two parts. The primary side of each scale is located on the right side of zero and is divided into full units of measurement, as in 1 mile, 1 foot, 1 kilometer, or 1 meter. On the left side of zero, you will find the extension scale, which is divided into tenths of the unit specified.

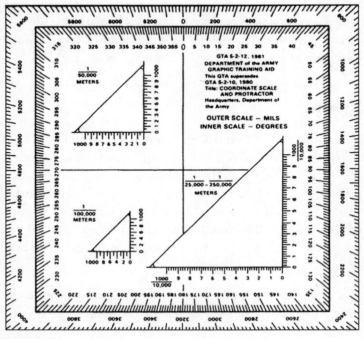

Example of a map scale

Measuring Straight-Line Distances

A compass with a clear base and numerical scale makes taking a straight-line map measurement an easy task. To eliminate confusion, make certain the numerical scale on the compass matches the numerical scale on the map or adjust for differences in scales.

A ruler or a simple piece of paper can also be used to measure distance. Here's how:

1. Measure the distance between two points, with the edge of a piece of paper or ruler touching both points on the map.

2. If using paper, use tick marks on the paper at these points. If using a ruler, record the distance on the ruler.

3. Move your paper or ruler down to the graphic bar scale. Align the right mark with a number on the primary side of the scale and the left mark with a number on the extension side of the scale. Remember, the primary side gives the distance in full units, while the extension side gives the remainder of the distance in tenths.

For example, if the distance between two points were 1.5 miles, the right-most mark would hit the 1-mile point on the primary side of the scale, while the left-most mark would reach the half-mile point on the extension side of the scale.

Measuring Curved Distances

When measuring the distance of a curved area, such as a road, a trail, or the distance around a lake, you'll need to use a variation of the method described above.

1. Make tick marks as needed along the route. Many marks may be needed, depending on the curve and length of the route.

2. Align the straight edge of a piece of paper so it touches the first and second marks you made on the map. Copy those marks onto the piece of paper.

3. Turn or pivot the paper's edge to touch the next point on the map, while leaving the last point you marked on the paper aligned with its corresponding point on the map. Mark this next point on the paper.

4. Continue this process until you have reached the destination marked on the map. Your final distance will be the measurement from the first mark on your paper to the last mark made.

The Basics of Map Coordinate Systems

In ordinary, everyday life, we take for granted how easy it is to explain to someone where to go for lunch, or where they can find you that evening for a meet up. Because we are so accustomed to our everyday surroundings, street signs, and buildings, giving directions is usually very simple. Most of the people in our lives are also familiar with the same areas. What would you do, though, if you were surrounded by unfamiliar mountains and you needed to give your location to someone else? What if you were in an area without your everyday landmarks and you, a loved one, or someone else you know required immediate medical attention? Would you have the ability to convey your exact location to a first responder with only your map? If you were given coordinates to meet up with others in your group, would you be able to pinpoint that location?

There is nothing more important in navigation than the ability to know exactly where you are, where you want to go, and how to get there. Once you have learned the basics of reading a map and understanding the symbols, it's time to move on to longitude, latitude, and the coordinate system.

Longitude and latitude can be represented in several different ways. Because topographical maps are the most commonly used maps by preppers and survivalists, we will focus on longitude and latitude as expressed in degrees, minutes, and seconds.

On any topographical map, you'll find lines of longitude and latitude. Longitudinal lines, also known as meridians, run north and south and provide coordinates for locations or objects on an east-to-west axis. The Prime Meridian, which passes through Greenwich, England, is represented as zero degrees longitude. As you travel east from zero degrees, the longitude increases up to 180 degrees east. Traveling west from zero degrees, the longitude is shown as a negative, down to −180 degrees west. While lines of longitude are positive or negative, they should always be given as east or west.

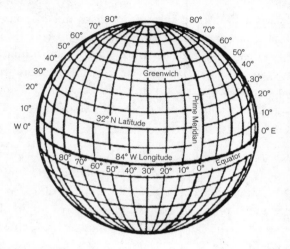

Longitude and latitude

Latitude lines run east to west, or parallel to the earth's Equator, and provide a coordinate for how far north or south of the Equator a place or object is. The Equator represents zero degrees. The farther north you go, the higher the number, eventually reaching 90° north (N). The farther south you travel from the Equator, the higher the number, eventually reaching 90° south (S). At the North Pole, the latitude would be read 90° N, and at the South Pole, it would be read 90° S. Because lines of latitude can have the same numerical value whether they are north or south of the Equator, the direction, N or S, must always be given.

At the Equator, one degree in longitude and latitude is approximately 70 miles. Lines of latitude are all equally spaced and the distance between them will remain the same. However, due to the contour of the earth, as you travel farther to the north or to the south, the lines of longitude will become closer together until they merge at the North or South Poles at 0 degrees.

While this type of map is popular, there are challenges to representing this curved system on a two-dimensional grid. Latitudinal lines are consistent between representation on a map and in distance on the earth's surface. Longitudinal lines, however, range from 70 miles per degree at the Equator to zero miles per degree at the poles. While still very practical for land navigation, the inconsistencies in scale make it less useful for navigational calculations.

Accuracy is increased on topographical maps by breaking down longitude and latitude into three parts: degrees, minutes, and seconds. One degree is equal to sixty minutes, and one minute is equal to sixty seconds. Here's an example of how you would write the exact location of Snow Lake, Idaho, using degrees (°), minutes ('), and seconds ('').

Latitude 48°38'36" N, Longitude: 116°35'46" W

On a topographical map, you will find lighter numbers running along the outside of the map. In each corner of the map will be the exact coordinates for longitude and latitude at that point, with additional numbers along the top and bottom for longitude, and along the left and right side of the map representing latitude. You'll also see darker, smaller numbers running along the edges. These are called UTMs, or Universal Transverse Mercator coordinates, and are most commonly used by the military, surveyors, or researchers.

It's well worth the very small investment if you don't already have a topographical map. In a very short time, you'll learn and understand the meaning of degrees, minutes, seconds, and those exact coordinates given at particular points along the map's edges and corners. You'll quickly learn to read and understand the meaning of contour lines, elevations, and the symbols provided. With this knowledge, you'll have the ability to navigate unknown areas with confidence, and you'll be able to relate to others your exact location, or that of any person or object, anywhere on the map.

THE COMPASS

The compass is an essential tool if you want to ensure your survival in the wilderness and successfully navigate your surroundings. With both the topographical map and the compass, you have the tools to reach any plausible destination. To develop the necessary skills of compass navigation, you must first learn the basic components, maintenance, and handling of a compass.

A good compass for both handheld and map navigation should have the following elements:

- transparent baseplate

- ruler, in inches

- magnetic needle, with north indicated in red

- compass wheel

- orienting lines

- direction-of-travel arrow

- declination scale

- index line

- degree dial, with incremental gradations
- United States Geological Survey (USGS) map scale

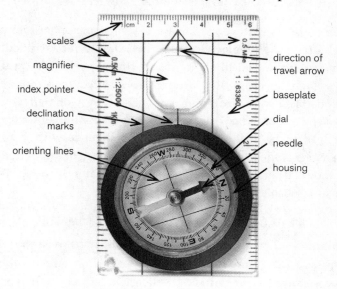

scales
magnifier
index pointer
declination marks
orienting lines

direction of travel arrow
baseplate
dial
needle
housing

The primary working components of a compass are the floating magnetic needle and the bezel ring, or compass wheel. The red end of the magnetic needle always points to the earth's magnetic North Pole, and the compass wheel, marked with N-S-E-W and degree marks, is used to set your bearing.

Care and Maintenance

A magnetic compass is a precision instrument that can be damaged easily. Damage and improper care can cause inaccurate readings. Computers and other electrical devices create magnetic fields, and exposure to these magnetic fields can damage a compass. Never store your compass near a heater or leave it in the car on a hot day, as prolonged exposure to excessive heat may also result in poor performance. Also, be sure that your compass isn't exposed to cell phones, radios, or other electrical devices. Cell phone speakers can demagnetize the needle of a compass, rendering it useless. Finally, avoid impacts between the compass and hard surfaces.

When outdoors with your compass, several common magnetic metal objects and electrical sources should be avoided. Nonmagnetic metals like aluminum, tin, copper, lead, and alloys such as brass and bronze won't affect a compass. Precious metals are also nonmagnetic, so they won't affect a compass. Here are some common things you may find outdoors that need to be avoided to prevent interference with your compass. Included is the recommended distance of separation that should be maintained between the object and the compass to ensure reliable, accurate readings.

COMMON OBJECTS THAT INTERFERE WITH A COMPASS

Object	Recommended Separation Distance
High-tension power lines	200 feet
Trucks, cars, or other vehicles	60 feet
Telephone wires and barbed wire	30 feet
Rifles or handguns	5 feet

Using the Compass

Anyone experienced in navigating the outdoors will tell you the compass may be your most valuable asset. It's actually quite simple to learn how to use a compass correctly, and it takes little time to become an expert. Learning to use a compass is a skill that any prepper, survivalist, hiker, backpacker, hunter, or outdoor enthusiast should know, although chances are, like most outdoor enthusiasts, you may already have a compass but are not taking advantage of all its advantages.

To find your bearing, hold the compass level in your hand with the direction arrow pointing away from you, toward the direction you want to travel. Next, turn the compass wheel until its north (N) lines up with the red end of the magnetic needle. You can now see at which bearing you are traveling.

True North and Magnetic North

The geographic North Pole, which is earth's true north, is at the top of the globe where you would expect it to be. This is where all lines of longitude meet. True north, represented on most maps by a star, is also north according to the earth's axis. This is the point from which you can determine your bearing. Maps also display vertical and horizontal grid lines, which are referred to as grid north and may be symbolized by the letters GN or the letter Y. These grid lines divide a map into squares to form a grid, and by using this grid, any point on the map may be located by a system of rectangular coordinates. However, the compass orients itself according to magnetic north (MN), which is about 250 miles away from true north, and constantly moves around due to changes in the earth's magnetic field. The difference between magnetic north and true north is the angle of declination. If you do not adjust your compass reading for this angle of declination you will miss your intended destination. The farther you travel the more off course you will become.

Anyone with just a little knowledge can move around an area successfully with just a compass. However, it's imperative to understand and incorporate declination when plotting an exact course or when using a map in conjunction with a compass. Before you can attempt to set an accurate bearing with your compass, you must first know your angle of declination.

Adjusting for Declination

Declination is the difference in angle between any two norths. Because the earth's magnetic field changes depending on your location, a declination scale with the value of declination is usually provided on a topographical map of that area. It is important to note that because of the changes in the earth's magnetic field, topo maps are updated every few years to reflect these changes. It is better to use the most current map available when navigating. The declination value displayed represents the error between magnetic north, grid north, and true north. When using a map and compass, the difference between magnetic and true north will be of most interest to you when adjusting for declination.

Declination values or degrees can be shown as easterly and westerly, or as positive and negative. Easterly declinations are represented as positive values, and westerly declinations are represented as negative values. As an example, your current location could be represented as a westerly declination of 10 degrees, or as a declination value of -10 degrees or -10 degrees.

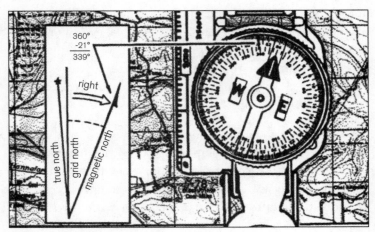

Adjusting for a westerly declination

Once you have found the declination value and scale on your map, usually located at the bottom, check to see if it is easterly or westerly. If you see magnetic north to the right of the true north line, it is an easterly declination. If you see magnetic north to the left of the true north line, it is a westerly declination. When setting your bearing, you must add or subtract the value between magnetic north and true north from your compass reading. The larger the declination value and the farther you travel without compensating for declination, the greater the likelihood of your running off course.

Let's look at a few examples to help you understand how to obtain the correct declination reading and adjust for declination on a compass.

Example: If you're aiming to travel a course with a bearing of 70° and the declination value of your location is 15°E (+15°), you are actually bearing at 85°. To travel at the correct bearing of 70°, you must set your compass to a bearing of 55° degrees, allowing for the 15° declination.

Example: If you're on a bearing of 90° and your location has a declination value of 12°E (+12°) your bearing will actually be at 78° degrees if you don't adjust for declination. To travel the correct bearing of 90°, set your compass to a bearing of 102°, having added the 12°.

Example: With a declination value of 10°W (-10°) and on a bearing of 80°, you would set your compass to a bearing of 70°, allowing for the -10° declination.

Remember to always keep your maps updated, as the earth's magnetic field changes over time, along with the declination angle.

Orienting a Map

Remember that when orienting a map, the compass must first be adjusted for the declination according to the declination scale at the bottom of the map.

1. With the map positioned horizontally on the ground or any relatively flat, smooth surface, place your adjusted compass on the map so the straight edge of the base plate is aligned with a north/south grid line on the map.

2. Turn the compass wheel until due north is aligned with the index pointer (the direction-of-travel arrow).

3. Rotate both map and compass together until the compass needle reads the degree of declination, as shown in the declination scale.

Having the map oriented, you can now pick out distant features like lakes, rivers, roads, or mountains in any direction and see these features in the same direction on the map. See Chapter 6 for more on terrain association.

MOVEMENT AND ROUTES

Occasionally I've considered myself a wanderer, spending a weekend in the mountains behind my home without a map or compass. I've hiked for hours, following game trails, foraging, and time permitting, maybe even doing a little fishing in one of the higher lakes. For me, this is as relaxing as it gets. I know every stream, lake, ridge, and giant pine within a 3-mile radius.

However, there was a time I would have never considered just wandering without my map and compass. I still would never step outside my 3-mile comfort zone without a map or compass. This book can be a great help even when you're in your comfort zone, and may save your life when you're traveling in unknown areas.

As a prepper, survivalist, or adventurer, the chances are high that you'll find yourself having to leave your comfort zone and travel in unfamiliar places. In order to move around successfully and safely, you must have an objective, a plan, and a route.

Having a map and knowing where you are at all times is essential. In this chapter, you'll learn how to use your map to place yourself in your terrain. You can discover where you are relative to your directional orientation and which way is north, south, east, and west. Along with directional orientation comes the confidence in the route you are taking and an understanding of the distance to your destination. Study and know the landmarks and features that surround you and learn them as they appear on the map. Look for impassible terrain features, such as rivers or cliffs. Examine the advantages and disadvantages of the terrain between where you are and where you want to be.

Resection

Resection is the method used to discover your location on the map by using two well-defined locations as reference points. Using three or more locations that can be found on the map will give greater accuracy.

1. Start by orienting the map in front of you with the compass.

2. Look into the distance and find two or three locations on the ground that you can also recognize on the map. Mark those locations on the map.

3. Using your compass, find the bearing from your current position to one of the locations.

4. Transfer this bearing to your properly oriented map by using a straight edge and drawing a line from the known location back to your current unknown location.

5. Repeat this process for the second position and a third, if available, for better accuracy. The point where these lines intersect represents your location.

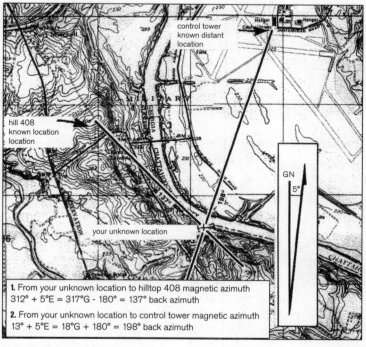

Resection on a topo map

Modified Resection

If you're walking along a linear feature that appears on the map, such as a road, fence line, or stream or canal, a modified resection can be done to find your position.

1. Orient the map as before, using a compass or terrain association.

2. Find a distant point that can be identified on both the ground and on the map.

3. Using your compass, determine the azimuth (bearing) to the distant known point.

4. Transfer this azimuth to the map by drawing a line from the known object back to your unknown grid location.

The point where the line crosses the linear feature on the map indicates your location.

Plan Your Route

The shortest distance between you and your destination isn't always the fastest. When possible, take advantage of terrain that is easier to walk. Sticking to friendly terrain may require you cover a little more distance but it will be easier and safer, and it may even shorten your overall travel time.

Use checkpoints to stay on track. The best checkpoints are usually linear crossings along your route, including railroads, streams, ridges, valleys, power lines, and paved roads. When using your map, use caution when relying on non-natural objects or vegetation as checkpoints. Too often, these features have changed since the map was produced. Watch out for obstacles that may require detours. Travel along ridges and valley floors whenever possible. These features offer easy travel and make good checkpoints. Working with the terrain is much easier than fighting it.

Before setting out on your planned route, review the map and the course to be taken. Take notice of areas where mistakes are likely to be made. Mark the map, or write notes at checkpoints or where changes of direction occur. Stay alert so you can watch for and recognize problem features while walking. As you travel, compare what you see in front of you with the course you laid out on the map. With each new route, take the time to plan again. Good planning will save time and grief.

Reach Your Destination

Quite often, the destination you have planned may be near an easy-to-recognize feature like a road crossing, cliff face, or lake. However, there will be times when obvious landscape features are not available. When traveling a long time in an unfamiliar territory without pronounced features to guide you, it's more likely an error may occur. One small error when many are possible can throw you off your planned route before reaching your destination.

You can eliminate the chances for error by using as many reference points as possible along your route, especially as you get closer to your final destination. In essence, break your planned route down into segments, or legs, using these points and features as intermediate destinations. Keep to your course by moving from one checkpoint to another, using the terrain and compass as guides. After reaching your last checkpoint, follow your compass while pacing off the remainder of what should be a relatively short distance to your final destination.

Navigating at Night

Because you'll have limited or no visibility, navigating at night has its own difficulties to overcome. Success while navigating at night depends on paying more attention to particular details during the planning stage. While the principles are the same as those of daytime navigation, compass headings in terrain hidden by darkness and for long distances require more thought and consideration.

In some cases, using the stars to navigate may serve you well, but a good understanding of the constellations and the location of stars is required. You can determine the four cardinal directions with the shadow-tip method (see page 12) if the moon is bright enough to cast a shadow.

Seeing in the Dark

Navigating at night, especially under cloud cover or on moonless nights, normally requires special equipment. There are a number of artificial light sources available to aid the navigator who needs to travel at night. But how do you find your way when batteries run out and equipment is damaged, or worse, forgotten? Several techniques can help you improve your natural nighttime vision.

Many years ago, I survived an accident that took away approximately 75 percent of my peripheral vision. While not causing total blindness, it did leave me learning how to see again with what vision I had remaining. What I learned was quite amazing. Not only was I able to learn how to see in a different way, but I also unknowingly improved my night vision several times over. While researching the topic for this book, I discovered that I had taught myself many of the following techniques years ago. You'll find many of these techniques quite simple and most, if not all, invaluable in nighttime land navigation—and even in everyday life.

Strengthen your peripheral vision. The eye retina contains two different types of photoreceptor cells that allow you to see: the cones and the rods. The cone cells are sensitive to color, while the rods see black and white. The rods also act as motion detectors and work better in low light. To see better in the darkness, you need to learn how to make the most of the rod cells and learn how to quickly manipulate your eyes so they can adapt to sudden changes in light. This is where peripheral vision comes in. To see the dimmest object, never look directly at it; instead, find that object in your peripheral vision, out of the corner of your eye.

When I lost most of my peripheral vision in the accident, I found the following exercise the greatest factor in strengthening what remained of my vision. Not only was I able to greatly improve the vision I had, it also made me astoundingly aware of my surroundings. While I still have considerable blind spots, I can see much more than I ever had in the areas of my vision that were not affected.

Strengthen your peripheral vision by sitting outside in an active area that you aren't already familiar with. A park bench on a Sunday, or even a busy street corner, would work well for this exercise. Find an object directly in front of you and focus on that object. Without looking in any other direction, take mental notes of all the objects that you can still see surrounding you, both moving and stationary. After making your mental list, relax, look around, and see what you missed. Repeat this exercise but in a different location, always trying to reach further into your peripheral vision.

Start seeing red. The rod cells in your eyes do not see the color red. Before going out into the darkness, wear red-tinted glasses or goggles for 20 to 30 minutes. This will enable you to see hidden objects and detect motion around you more quickly. By blocking out everything in the visual spectrum except the color red, your eyes will adjust to the darkness easier and faster.

Block out all light.[7] Bright sunlight and ultraviolet radiation from the sun will reduce your ability to adjust to darkness. Wear sunglasses during daytime travel. For every two to three hours the eyes are exposed to bright sunlight, adjusting to the darkness can be delayed by about ten minutes. In addition, wearing sunglasses during the day will increase how well you see at night. Even exposing your eyes to sunlight for 10

---

7 Theodore Leng, MD, reviewer, "How to See in the Dark," *WikiHow*, Accessed Jan. 2017, http://www.wikihow.com/See-in-the-Dark.

consecutive days without sunglasses can reduce your night vision by as much as 50 percent. Sunglasses that have neutral gray lenses that will allow 15 percent or less of visible light are recommended.

If you have a moon overhead, try to avoid looking at it or any other light source. That means don't light that cigarette, if you smoke. The more light you expose your eye to, the smaller the pupil will get. In dark or low light conditions, the idea is to have the pupil open as wide as possible and have it remain open. If you have to look at a light source (for example, if you need to stop and study a map with a match or penlight), cover one eye until you're through.

Acclimate to the darkness. Before venturing out of your shelter or leaving the campfire at night, adjust your night vision by closing or covering your eyes for 20 to 30 minutes. Wearing an eye patch before entering a dark area is a good technique. By protecting one eye for 20 to 30 minutes, you will be able to walk in a darkened area with that eye already accustomed to the darkness.

Don't rely on what's in front of you. Eyes have natural blind spots that can be avoided when navigating through darkness by utilizing peripheral vision. Focus on the sides of objects and when walking through dark areas, look away from the center of your direction of travel. Your peripheral vision will identify shapes and detect movements much better than your forward vision.

Look for silhouettes and contrasts. By bending down or keeping as low to the ground as possible, you'll find that the light that does come from the night sky will make more objects visible. The light source will appear to come from above or behind objects, creating a contrasting shadow or silhouette on the ground. While the rods in your eyes can only discriminate between black and white, they are far more sensitive than the cones and can detect these shadows more easily. This technique of creating silhouettes will provide you with useful images.

Massage your eyes. Close your eyes. Then, with the palms of your hands, apply light pressure while massaging your eyes. After 5 or 10 seconds, the blackness will turn to white then fade back to black. When you reopen your eyes, you'll see better in the darkness. Another method is to simply squeeze your eyes very tight for 5 to 10 seconds when entering a dark area, and then reopen them. You'll find similar results to the massage method.

Be alert and use all your senses while traveling at night. As the ability to use one of your senses decreases, nature will increase the ability of other senses. Listen for sounds like running water and the wind through bushes and trees. While your eyes are adjusting, move slowly with arms outstretched and use touch to guide you. While real navigation may stop in total darkness, the ability to use your senses to detect objects around you will help keep you safe.

DEAD RECKONING

Several years ago, a high school buddy and I were snowmobiling just outside of Bend, Oregon, when we experienced a complete whiteout. It was an overcast day with just a light snowfall and visibility was good, but at the drop of a hat, that all changed. As hard as it may be to imagine, we could not see the big pine trees less than 15 feet away, let alone the forest itself. There was no up or down, and the sense of vertigo and falling was overwhelming. We were not prepared for such an event, and neither of us had a compass. Fortunately, the whiteout we experienced lasted only a short time, maybe 20 minutes.

Dead reckoning is the process of calculating one's current position by using a previously determined location and advancing to that location based on known or estimated speeds over elapsed time and course. Dead reckoning, along with a map and compass, can be used across open country and is a common technique used in navigation when terrain association is limited and visibility is low. It's useful in dense forests and areas hit with heavy rain, fog, or snow. Because of sparse terrain, non-natural obstacles, and uncertain safety, most movements by dead reckoning won't follow a straight-line distance to a checkpoint. Dead reckoning may consist of several short, straight-line legs between different checkpoints. Without the help of terrain association, the increased distance between checkpoints increases the chance of errors. Traveling along shorter, straight-line distances and trying to stay on or parallel to roads or trails will reduce these errors.

Never walk with the compass held out in front of you when following a specified azimuth across open land during daylight. When used this way, the compass cannot stay steady or level and won't give you accurate readings. From your start point, face a landmark that is located along your desired azimuth and align the compass. Match up your compass as often as needed to complete the straight-line segment of the route.

The advantage to dead reckoning is that the technique is relatively simple. Another advantage is that it can be a very accurate way of moving from one point to another if the distances are short and care is taken in planning.

Walking Distance and Time

Bob plans to meet up with Jack, Bill, Susan, and the rest of the hunting party, but he wonders if he has time to see if there are any fish biting in the stream near his camp. He reflects on the rules of walking distance and time, and calculates how long it will take him to reach the others.

Knowing your pace count, based on your natural step, is extremely important when you're dead reckoning. The average person has a natural step of 30 inches, but this can vary depending on several factors. Height, body weight, and physical health will all affect your natural step. To determine your natural step, mark off a distance that's easy for you to use and remember. For example, if you're comfortable judging the distance of 100 yards, walk that distance to learn the number of steps it takes you to get there.

The average walking speed for an individual is about 5.6 miles per hour (5 kilometers per hour) but, like your natural step, this can also vary depending on body weight, height, and physical condition. You first have to know your own pace before you can confidently judge the time it will take you to get from where you are to your intended destination. To learn your pace, mark a straight one-mile or one-kilometer path on normal, flat ground. Walk this path with your natural step, in normal conditions, while timing yourself.

Once you know your natural step and the speed at which you walk, practice with consideration to variable conditions. Under a more natural outdoor environment, most conditions will slow your walking speed. There are many factors that need to be accounted for in judging distance and time, such as rain, snow, and winds; mud, sand, and uphill slopes; and the extra weight you may be carrying, like clothing, a backpack, and firearms. Even walks downhill, which in some cases could add to your walking speed, may be slowed due to deadfalls, brush, or other obstacles. With a little thought and practice, you'll be better able to judge the time it takes to reach your destination. Allow yourself room for error; it's always better to be early than miss your ride or be caught in the dark.

Steering Marks

These landmarks used in dead reckoning are more commonly known as steering marks. These steering marks should be selected during the course of travel, rather than from the map. They must be easily identifiable landmarks, such as hilltops, rock formations, or towers, and should be on or near visible high points along the azimuth line. If a good steering mark isn't visible from your location, you may be able to use a back azimuth (a bearing of 180° behind you; a complete reverse-course) to find a feature behind you until a good steering mark appears out in front.

If you have more than one easily identifiable steering mark, choose the one that is farthest away. This will allow you to travel farther while making fewer references to the compass. A taller or higher mark may be the best choice if it can be more easily seen without getting lost in the background of the terrain you're following.

As day turns to night, colors turn to grays and blacks, and steering marks disappear in the darkness. Concentrate more on the most unique shapes. Remember that they will be seen more as outlines and that as you walk they will appear to change, depending on the angle you view them from.

Bypassing an Obstacle

While traveling a predetermined course with a compass, you may need to deviate due to an unexpected river, rock formation, or other obstacle. You can normally bypass an obstacle by moving around it at 90-degree angles and tracking your distance. This method can also be used at night.

1. If you're going north, use the direction arrow on your compass to turn your body 90 degrees until the compass needle aligns to either east (left turn) or west (right turn), depending on the direction you choose to bypass the object.

2. Start walking in the direction indicated by the compass. Count the number of steps it takes for you to move across the face of the obstacle.

3. Once you're past the front of the obstacle, turn your body 90 degrees back to your original bearing and continue walking until you reach the end of the obstacle.

4. To get back on course, turn your body in the opposite direction from which you initially deviated. For example, if you originally turned east to pass the face of the obstacle, you should now turn west.

5. Remember how many steps you took to cross the face of the obstacle. Pace-count that many steps to get past the object, and stop.

6. Using the direction arrow on your compass, turn your body to face your original heading, and continue on your path.

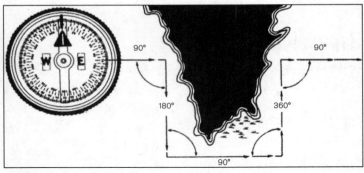

Bypassing an obstacle

If you're in a group of two or more people, have one member of your group advance around the obstacle. Once this member is on the other side, use verbal or hand signals to position the member into a direct line between you and your compass heading. Once the member is in place and stationary, you can move to his location and continue your course.

Making Your Move

When traveling alone, first determine your location on the map, the distance to your planned destination, and your compass bearing toward your objective. Once your azimuth is set on your compass, turn your body in the direction you want to travel and start walking. Keep track of your pace count while following your bearing, making sure the north-seeking arrow on the compass stays aligned until you reach your destination. Rough terrain, bad weather, and poor visibility can all affect your pace count. The further the objective, the greater the chances for error, so break the planned route down into legs and use checkpoints whenever possible.

When planning a dead reckoning movement, use linear checkpoints to keep you on course. Rivers, streams, valleys, ridges, and paved roads all make good checkpoints because they can usually be seen on the map and may intersect your planned course. Be careful when using non-natural objects that have been marked on your map, such as dirt roads, trails, or fences. Time, lack of use, Mother Nature, or human intervention can cause these landmarks to change—some may even completely disappear. Natural areas are not immune to change, either. A forest shown on a map may have been logged, and a clearing may now be overgrown.

To choose your checkpoints, look on the map for what appear to be the most permanent features, then measure and jot down the distances. As you pace-count and come close to the checkpoints, slow down and take the time to recognize them. If you find your checkpoint, make a note on your map and continue on to the next. If you cannot find your checkpoint, do not proceed to the next unless you're sure you won't miss it. If you feel you may be lost, set your compass for a reverse course of 180 degrees and pace-count back to your previous checkpoint. Study your map again for the checkpoint and distance. Find your error, if there is one, or look for a better possible checkpoint.

Dead Reckoning and the Point Person

Even at night, when visibility is at its worst, land navigation and movement is still possible—that is, if you're not alone. If you have two or more people in your party, at least one of whom has some experience and a compass, you can implement a point person to guide you in the absence of recognizable landscape features.

The point person acts as the group's reference point, trekking out in front of the designated navigator but remaining close enough to stay visible and communicate verbally, with the use of hand signals, or with a flashlight. The point person starts out on an agreed-upon course in a general direction. Then, when a comfortable distance is reached, the navigator signals a stop. The navigator then signals the point person to move in the proper direction, which will align the point person with the compass heading. Once the point person is in place, the navigator can now move to meet the person while maintaining the path to the desired checkpoint or destination.

Multiple Point People

With a larger group that has several people experienced in using a compass, the process of using a navigator and a point person can be sped up. With the designated navigator maintaining a position, two or more in the group may take the point. As before, the navigator has complete control in directing people to the positions required to maintain an accurate heading. Once those who will take the point are in the correct line of bearing, the point person farthest from the navigator will assume the role of the new navigator and direct the others to the next point. The original navigator can now move forward to the first point man or new navigator.

A word of caution: Because each individual has a unique step or pace count, distance estimates can be affected. The first navigator must be the only one to keep pace count as he moves forward to each point person to minimize error. Also, keep in mind that this process of navigation may require taking shorter steps due to surrounding conditions, and that these additional steps must be considered when estimating the total steps needed to get to the end destination.

Handrails and Catching Points

When dead reckoning over long distances, an alert navigator will often find help and eliminate errors by using a compass and taking assistance from the terrain.

Handrails are linear features that run parallel to your direction of travel. Roads, power lines, streams, ridgelines, or railroads can all be used to help navigate, as long as the feature travels with you on your right or left side. These features allow you to rough compass, or estimate your bearing, without having to use steering marks or precision compass work.

When referencing the map, find the spot where you see your route or handrail change direction. Select a prominent feature near this point to provide a warning. This feature, called a catching point, will also tell you when you have gone too far. This catching point also indicates where area navigation should end and point navigation should begin.

TERRAIN ASSOCIATION

Preppers, survivalists, and weekend adventurers can increase the odds of successful navigation using the vast amounts of information provided on the map and the corresponding features that the eye sees on the ground. The more time spent studying and using a map, the easier it becomes to visualize the terrain, quickly correct errors by recognizing visible landmarks, and estimate distances. Knowing and practicing these skills would make anyone an invaluable asset to a group.

If you're not sure where you are on a map, orientation by map terrain can help give you a general idea and at times can be very accurate. Upon seeing two or more features in the distance and recognizing them on the map, you can judge where you are by comparison. As an example, say you look out into the distance and see a mountain north of your position and a lake to the west. Then, you recognize them both on the map. You can follow an imaginary line south of the mountain, while at the same time following an imaginary line east of the lake. Two lines will intersect at your general location.

Careful examination of the map and the ground, or terrain association, is an invaluable technique when a compass isn't available or quick reference is required.

There are five major terrain features represented by the detail of contour lines on a topographical map: hilltop, valley, ridge, depression, and saddle. Match these features on the map with the same features on the ground. In terrain where verifying features is more difficult, keep checking your map; it's always the determining factor.

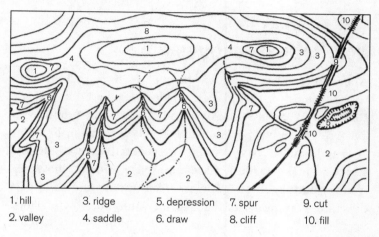

| 1. hill | 3. ridge | 5. depression | 7. spur | 9. cut |
| 2. valley | 4. saddle | 6. draw | 8. cliff | 10. fill |

Vegetation and Water Features

Topographical maps will often show vegetation as symbols such as orchards or vineyards, and it's important for the user to be familiar with these symbols as they appear in the legend. When comparing vegetation as depicted on a topographical map to that seen on the ground, it's also important to consider what might have changed. Vegetation features can change overnight due to the influence of Mother Nature and of man. Forest fires, logging, land development, and farming are just a few of the things that could occur and change the appearance of the landscape from what is seen on the map.

The shapes and sizes of lakes and reservoirs can be very useful for orienting yourself to location; also helpful are rivers, streams, and their direction of flow. As with vegetation, these features can also change, but their changes are less likely or less noticeable under normal circumstances. However, depending on time of year and location, change may be more prevalent. In spring after a winter thaw, bodies of water may appear larger due to snowmelt or rain, as opposed to their late summer or fall appearances. Winter conditions, snow, and ice may hide these features altogether.

Non-Natural Features

Almost anywhere in the world you go, humans have been there. In most of these places, they left some kind of mark. Non-natural features such as roads, power lines, buildings, and bridges are usually shown as symbols that can be found on map legends. These symbols are generally easy to identify and can make terrain association very simple; however, like vegetation, these landmarks can appear and disappear depending on the age of the map and other unknown factors.

Different Seasons, Different Terrain

Depending on where you are, seasons can be distinct, and in some cases, extreme. The change in terrain will usually become more evident with a more noticeable change in seasons.

In winter, as mentioned earlier, bodies of water change quite noticeably. Traces of vegetation may be all that's seen due to snowfall. What once stood out may be all but invisible; however, mountains, ridges, valleys, and saddles will normally become very distinct.

During spring, early summer, or the rainy season, excess moisture due to snowmelt and rainfall will lead to an increase in the growth of vegetation. Often, this growth will make it more difficult to recognize terrain features. Ponds and streams may swell to look like lakes and rivers. Not only can this swelling change the appearance of bodies of water, but it may also cause secondary runoffs or streams that do not appear on maps. Erosion in areas where vegetation is sparse also changes the contour and shape of the land.

7

TERRAIN COMPARISON AND NAVIGATION

In the past few chapters, we covered the basics of navigation that can be used on land anywhere in the world. What about those environments with special or extreme conditions? Odds are, you've experienced an extreme condition and likely will experience one again. Hopefully your last experience was a pleasant one, without unwanted surprises. Let's take a look at considerations and useful ideas that will help if you find yourself in an undesirably extreme environment.

The Desert

When we hear the word desert, most of us envision a vast area of rolling sand dunes, clear skies, and hot temperatures. When you look up the word desert you will find what seems an endless number of definitions. Classifications usually rely on some combination of the number of days of rainfall, total amount of annual rainfall, humidity, temperature, and other factors. In 1953, American geographer Peveril Meigs divided desert regions on Earth into three categories based on the amount of precipitation they received; this is now a widely accepted system by many geologists and the USGS. Extremely arid lands have at least 12 consecutive months without rainfall, arid lands receive less than 250 millimeters of annual rainfall, and semiarid lands have a mean annual precipitation of between 250 and 500 millimeters. Arid and extremely arid lands are deserts, and semiarid grasslands generally are referred to as steppes (grasslands void of trees, except those near rivers or streams).

Fraser Cain of *Universe Today* tells us "deserts actually make up 33 percent, or one third, of the land's surface area."[8] The percentage of desert land in the United States, though less than one third of the planet, is still vast. Here in the United States, there are four major deserts: the Great Basin, Mojave, Sonoran, and Chihuahuan Deserts.

Terrain varies in desert regions depending on your location. When most people think of a desert, they imagine a large expanse of sand, rolling dunes, and high heat; however, a desert can also include lava beds, salt flats, and mountain ranges of barren hills. Even arctic regions, where temperatures always remain cold, are considered desert.

Finding your way through a desert region can present difficulties to anyone not frequently exposed to this type of environment. Temperatures can reach above 115°F during the day, producing the need to do most navigation at night using the stars. Deserts of sand will generally have dunes that align themselves into specific patterns caused by prevailing winds. As an example, prevailing winds from either the west or east will shape the dunes into a north-south pattern. The shadow-

---

8 Fraser Cain, "What Percentage of the Earth's Land Is Desert?" *Universe Today*, December 24, 2015, Accessed Jan. 2017, http://www.universetoday.com/65639/what-percentage-of-the-earths-land-surface-is-desert.

tip method can also be used to estimate north. The lack of trees and other features prevent comparisons, so this must be considered in observations when judging distance.

Desert and Water

Survival in desert navigation is closely associated with animals, vegetation, landscape, and water. Watch for animal tracks or paths; those leading downhill will often lead to water. A group of animals is a high indicator that water is close by. Songbirds or birds circling an area may also be an indicator of nearby water. If you come across flies or swarms of mosquitoes, look for water in that area.

An abundance of vegetation will generally mean nearby water or water slightly belowground surface. Depending on your area, look for the greenest plants and those with larger leaves, as these generally require more water.

Canyons and valleys shaded in the heat of the day may be hiding water. Moisture from earlier snowfalls or rain are more likely to be retained in these shaded areas, even months after a major rainfall. Look for depressions in dry streams or riverbeds. In Chapter 11, we'll talk more about procuring water.

Desert Navigation

Land navigation in broad desert basins or rocky plateaus usually requires traversing a wide expanse without several terrain features to help guide your movement. Relying on a single feature at a great distance can cause problems, unless you frequently confirm your location by resection or utilizing nearby features. Use closer features whenever possible to confirm your location and reduce errors. A small checkpoint or objective can be missed by several kilometers when using features at a great distance.

In sandy or dune deserts, visual clues may be limited. High winds creating sand storms or darkness will also limit visibility. When these conditions exist, navigation by dead reckoning, as explained in Chapter 5, must be used. When applying these techniques, understanding special conditions, such as sudden drops in elevation or hidden obstacles, will be extremely helpful.

Most desert conditions can be related to high temperatures, which lead to excessive loss of body moisture. Depending on the length of time that might be required to reach your destination and the amount of water you have, consider nighttime navigation, using either the stars or dead reckoning.

Mountain Terrain

Generally understood to be larger than hills, mountains are usually found as ranges, elongated or in circular groups. Because contour lines generally show prominent ridges, high peaks, steep slopes, and large valleys, identifying mountains and navigating these areas using the map is usually very easy. Still, care must be taken in the study of the map and terrain before setting a course. While prominent features make navigation easy, altitude, high peaks, steep slopes, and snow can all hinder and make some routes dangerous.

Due to higher elevations, mountain conditions are usually colder and wetter than you might expect. Wind speeds should also be accounted for, as they will increase the effect of the cold. Visibility may also be limited due to the greater likelihoods of snow, rain, and fog. However, in good weather, the elevations of mountainous terrain offer excellent long-range views.

Mountainous terrain at first glance may appear to offer little in the way of shelter from adverse weather. But if weather or fatigue dictates a need for shelter, look for rocky outcroppings, boulders, and heavy vegetation.

Mountain Navigation

The best and usually the easiest routes for movement in mountain terrain will be roads and trails. Otherwise, the techniques discussed earlier are valid options.

When traveling a slope, either straight up or straight down, determine the relationship of the top of the slope or ridgeline to the slope. Take a compass reading along an imaginary line that runs straight up and down the slope. This compass reading will cut through the contour lines as shown on your map at about a 90-degree angle. By checking the map and knowing the direction of slope where you are located, you will be able to keep track of your location. As with desert navigation, understanding the terrain and special conditions will help you navigate and find your way.

If you know you'll be traveling in mountain conditions, an altimeter is a useful tool to have on hand. Like a barometer, an altimeter measures barometric pressure, but it takes measurements on an adjustable scale using feet or meters. With the use of the altimeter, you can pinpoint your position through resection. Instead of using two or more different directional values, you can use one directional value and one elevation value.

Jungle and Forest Terrain

It's unlikely that preppers or survivalists will find themselves in an actual jungle, but some of the following information can be used in similar terrains across the globe.

Jungles are large geographic regions located within the tropics on or near the Equator. You can expect to find jungles in Central America, Southeast Asia, Africa, India, and along the Amazon River. Known for rainy, humid areas, jungles contain a wide variety of wildlife, such as alligators, monkeys, parrots, snakes, and tigers. The jungle is also home to a wide variety of insects that can carry diseases like cholera, malaria, and yellow fever. There are times when jungles are impenetrable due to the heavy layers of tangled vegetation. Because of the heavy foliage, navigation by terrain comparison can be very difficult. If lost in the jungle, you may eventually find your way back to civilization by following any body of water and its flow downstream. However, you may encounter potentially hostile civilizations who consider anyone not local to that area an intruder.

Jungle and Forest Conditions

Near the Equator, all seasons are nearly alike and receive large amounts of rain all year. Climate can vary farther from the Equator, with distinct wet and dry seasons. Whether near or far from the Equator, annual rainfall can exceed 400 inches, with a constant high humidity of 90 percent all year. Temperatures average 75°F to 95°F, but the heat can seem exasperated by the high humidity.

Typical to the jungle environment are cultivated areas, dense forests, grasslands, and swamps. Based upon the vegetation and terrain, forests are classified as either primary or secondary. Primary forests include tropical rain forests and broadleaved (deciduous) forests. Secondary forests are generally overgrown with grasses, thorns, weeds, canes, and shrubs, and can be found at the edge of rain forests, deciduous forests, and in areas where jungles have been cleared and abandoned. Visibility in a secondary forest is severely limited because of thick vegetation that can grow over six feet high.

Large trees make up the majority of the tropical rain forest. Branches crisscross each other, forming two or three canopies at different levels above the ground. Because the canopies shield the jungle floor from sunlight, there will be less undergrowth; however, it's common to find aboveground root systems and hanging vines. Visibility is generally limited to about 150 feet.

In the semitropical zones where there are both wet and dry seasons, you'll find deciduous forests. In the wet season, trees are fully leafed, while in the dry season, most of this foliage dies. Trees are usually less dense here than in the rain forests, allowing more sunlight and producing more undergrowth. Visibility and movement is limited, but this improves during the dry season.

Swamps are common in all jungle areas where there is poor drainage, and any land navigation requires careful study of the map and the ground. There are two main types of swamps, mangrove and palm, and navigation of these areas usually calls for dead reckoning. Found in coastal areas wherever tides influence water flow, mangroves are shrub-like trees that can grow as high as 18 feet. Mangroves have a tangled root system both above and below the water, which makes movement difficult.

Savannas, or grassy plains, occur within the tropics but are generally located away from the Equator. The vegetation in these flatlands is much different from that of jungles. Savannas consist mainly of grasses that can grow to a height of over 12 feet. Shrubs and isolated trees are also common to the savanna. Tall grass, coupled with a few trees, can make dead reckoning or navigation by stars the only option. Cultivated areas, rice paddies, and plantations can also be found in the jungle, from well-planned, well-managed farms and plantations to smaller tracts of land kept by local farmers.

Jungle Navigation

Terrain association, near or far, is extremely limited in the jungle. Navigation in the jungle is usually limited to the compass and dead reckoning. There are few straight-line movements possible with jungle navigation, making navigation more difficult. When in this type of landscape, constant use of the compass and an accurate pace count is required.

The most common error in jungle navigation is overestimating the distance of travel. Considering the different types of terrain you may encounter during your walk, a personal pace count should be practiced and written down for each expected terrain. While relying on the use of a compass and dead reckoning, incorporate terrain association with short legs and point navigation until you reach your final destination.

Winter Terrain

Winter terrain navigation is much like arctic terrain navigation.[9] Since most readers of this book may be more familiar with the term winter conditions and navigation is relatively the same in both situations, the following suggestions apply to both.

Winter terrain can be associated with cold weather without snow, but for the purposes of this book, we will focus on conditions where there may be light to heavy snowfall and accumulation resulting in packed snow or frozen ground. While packed snow or frozen ground can make movement from one point to another relatively simple, accumulated or fresh snow can slow travel to a great degree, depending on the amount of snow and the terrain being traveled.

---

9 Headquarters, Department of the Army, "FM 3-25.26. Map Reading and Land Navigation," US Army, January 2005, Accessed Jan. 2017, http://www.globalsecurity.org/military/library/policy/army/fm/3-25-26/fm3-25-26_c1_2006.pdf.

Seasoned preppers and adventurers alike are generally prepared when expecting travel in winter conditions. Traveling through deep snow and cold weather requires special attention to your clothing and footwear.

Winter Navigation

If the possibility of winter navigation exists, then train or practice in similar conditions with special equipment like clothing, snowshoes, or skis. Pace count, distance measurement, and time tracking can change greatly in winter conditions, so these skills need to be practiced in appropriate conditions. Greater amounts of snow and colder temperatures can shorten a pace count by half and increase time of travel needed to reach a destination tremendously.

In snowy terrain, your ability to navigate at night will often be enhanced by light from the moon and stars reflecting off the snow. With visibility enhanced, it's likely that navigation by terrain association is possible. Even in cloudy conditions, winter nights may be brighter than a typical moonlit summer night, during which there is no snow and the ground is dark.

EXPOSURE AND TREATMENT WHILE NAVIGATING

I don't remember their names; it's been over 45 years. So I'll call these two fellows Tom and Jerry, like from the cartoon. It's fitting, because looking back now, the incident that took place and the details leading up to it were quite comical.

My dad, my uncle Marv, and I were on the north side of High Lake in eastern Oregon at about 7,000 feet, dressing an antelope my uncle had just bagged. While preparing the animal for the pack (trek) out, we discussed our options. It was still early, maybe 10:00 a.m., but it would require two trips and the better part of the day to carry out all the meat. The mountain had seen little snow so far, just a couple of inches, but the terrain was rough, and in places it was very steep. When we got back to camp, we would recruit my two brothers to help with the second trip.

As we were packing what we could carry, we heard Tom and Jerry coming up the mountain to the south of us. It was a bit of a surprise running into anyone where we were, even hunters; but we soon found out Tom and Jerry were not hunters.

They had not seen us yet, and we watched them as they struggled toward us through brush and deadfall. Tom was in the lead, an average-size man in his mid-twenties, I would guess. He was wearing insulated coveralls, hiking boots, and had a coat slung over his shoulder. He also had an air of certainty and authority that rang through as he barked unintelligible words over his shoulder to Jerry. Jerry was also somewhere in his mid-twenties, but that's where the resemblance stopped. Jerry was maybe 5'6" tall, and better than half that wide. He wore blue jeans, a long-sleeve shirt over a T-shirt, boots, and baseball cap. Jerry had a build that made you wonder how his pants stayed up. It was easy to see he was struggling to keep pace with Tom.

We watched in silence as they got closer, and I'm sure the three of us were all thinking the same thing: these boys are going to jump right out of their socks when they finally see us. At no more than 5 feet away, my dad said, "Hello, boys." If their boots had not been tied, I'm sure both would have left their socks when they heard his voice.

It's not often you come across other people where we were. The terrain is rough and the weather, while sometimes reaching the 40s and 50s during the day, can get extremely cold at night, often dropping down to well below freezing. Tom and Jerry were not hunters and carried no rifles, although Tom did have a side arm. Both were pleasant enough, but Jerry was definitely out of place. Five minutes into our visit, he was still breathing hard and sweating.

They told us they were on break from college on a hiking and camping weekend, and that they liked to adventure and practice survival skills. Jerry mostly listened as Tom told us about how, the year before, they camped in a snow cave on Mount Hood for a weekend. The more Tom talked, the more skeptical we became of their experience. Along with Tom's pistol, they also had a map of the area, water, waterproof matches, some food, and a knife, but little else.

We learned that Tom and Jerry were camped at Indian Spring Butte, which was not far; maybe a mile west of where we were and about a mile north of the main road. Their plan was to hike north to Strawberry Lake, then turn southeast, stopping at Strawberry Falls on the way back to Indian Spring Butte. At 16 years old but having hunted this area for several years, I thought their plan sounded simple enough. The entire trip would be about 6 miles, with most of it being downhill from where we now stood. My uncle thought different and so did my dad. The questions and warnings flew.

We asked them if anyone knew where they were going or when they'd be back. Did they have an emergency supply of food?

We informed Tom and Jerry that about 100 yards from where we were was nothing but loose shale, and even with what little snow there was, it would be better to go around it. Beyond the shale until they reached Little Strawberry Lake, a half mile or so from where we were, the forest was thick with trees, deadfall, and brush, so walking would be difficult.

My uncle, who worked part time with a mounted division of search and rescue in Oregon, knew the area well, and he estimated they wouldn't make it back to their camp until just before sunset —if they had no trouble at all. He recommended that if they wanted to go to the lake, they should turn back and start again in the morning, heading directly to the lake using the trail, without taking any detours, and returning following the same path.

We could tell that Jerry liked the idea of heading back to camp and starting over in the morning, if at all, but Tom was insistent that they wouldn't have any trouble and should continue on. Still concerned, we gave Tom and Jerry what we had left in the food we carried and wished them well. As they thanked us and headed out, my dad told them, "If you have any trouble, fire off three shots from that pistol of yours and sit tight. We'll come and look for you."

That day, we managed to get the entire antelope back to camp with plenty of daylight to spare. With a nice big fire going, we ate dinner, and talked about the day, Tom and Jerry, and the hunt for tomorrow. The stars were out by this point and the temperature was dropping pretty fast when we heard the gunshots—three shots, and nothing more. We had little doubt who had fired the shots, but they seemed to come from the southwest and were close by, not northwest toward Strawberry Lake, which was the direction Tom and Jerry were heading. If it was Tom and Jerry, as we suspected, they were nowhere near the area we expected them to be. They were also on their own until sometime tomorrow. One or both might have been hurt, but lost was more likely; however, there was no question that it was too late for us to go out, and nothing would be done that night. Hopefully they were not hurt, and their survival and fire-making skills were better than their navigation skills.

The next morning found us packed, ready to go, and waiting by the fire for enough daylight to head out. We would leave at daylight. My uncle and two brothers would head southwest, while my dad and I would go northwest. We would all converge on an old logging skid road that circled the mountain about halfway toward the top, and then we would head toward each other on that road to meet somewhere in the middle. If either party should come across the two adventurers, they were to fire three shots followed by two more to let the others know.

As daylight broke and we were about to leave, we heard three more shots. These three shots seemed to come from the same direction as before, southwest, but our plan remained the same. They made it through a very cold night—well, at least one of them did. Dad fired three shots in return and we headed up the mountain.

It took my dad and me about three hours to reach the old logging road, where we rested and listened. After a few minutes of hearing nothing, we began heading south. It wasn't much of a road, having not been used in years. Much of it was overgrown, and some parts were not even recognizable as a road. We figured it would take another two hours or so to meet up with my uncle and brothers.

We had not gone far down this road when we heard three more shots. It was still hard to guess how far away—maybe a mile, maybe two—but we were heading the right direction. Forty-five minutes or so had gone by when we heard the report of my brother's .30-06. The sound of his rifle was unmistakable. Three shots followed by two more: they had found Tom and Jerry.

We could smell the smoke before we saw the fire. My uncle, Tom, and Jerry were sitting near the fire while my brothers gathered more wood nearby. Both of the "real survivalists," as we began to refer to them, looked the worse for wear. Tom and Jerry were huddled nearest the fire, sharing a blanket that my uncle had brought wrapped around their backs and shoulders. They were physically exhausted and obviously had not slept the night before. Jerry's face and hands were scratched up pretty good, but nothing serious. Both were suffering from what appeared to be a mild case of hypothermia.

Water was heated over the fire, and after a struggle of eating sandwiches and drinking water, their shivers and chattering teeth began to subside. As they were warming up, our questions became easier to answer. Jerry did most of the talking; I think Tom was a bit more embarrassed than Jerry, and only interrupted on occasion to clarify. It actually seemed that Jerry was now excited about what had happened, not realizing how close they both came to dying up in the mountains.

Between a few more shivers and chattering teeth, we pretty much figured out what took place. They had skirted the shale area, heading north as we had suggested, but soon after they entered the heavy forest and thick undergrowth, Tom felt they had headed too far west and started to adjust their course toward the east. They both knew that an hour or so of hiking should have taken them clear of the heavy forest, but they were now into the hike almost two hours. Realizing his mistake in heading east, Tom changed course again, this time heading more westerly. He made his second mistake by overcompensating for his first. They were now somewhere just north of where we had met them the day before and were heading in a west-southwest direction. Eventually, Tom and Jerry came across the logging road we found them on and had absolutely no idea where they were. There was no sun, only gray, and it was getting dark, so they decided to follow the road for a while to see if it went anywhere. With nightfall coming, they stopped, built a fire, and fired the three shots we had heard.

Even without a compass, you would think that having a detailed map showing clear landmarks, checkpoints, and short distances in between these checkpoints would make it hard to get lost. However, when looking back, we had terrain that allowed little visibility, a sky that was overcast and showed little or no sun, and two adventurers with little experience. The whole ordeal could have been much worse. If they hadn't had the means to build a fire or hadn't faced the fact they were lost and then signaled for help, Tom and Jerry wouldn't have survived. While we were all able to walk back to camp that November, with the extremely cold nights we could easily have been packing out Tom and Jerry instead of an antelope.

STAY FIT

Land navigation almost always involves a great amount of physical exertion. If you're overweight, your body will have a harder time regulating its temperature in both cold and hot climates. Avoid alcohol, caffeine, and recreational drugs. Know your body and be aware of your limitations. A healthy body can travel through tough terrain easier, faster, and longer, covering a greater distance in a shorter amount of time. When traveling with others remember that your physical condition will either help or hinder the progress of the entire group.

Whenever planning a movement to a new destination, exposure to the elements and proper clothing to combat weather effects must be considered. People often think about the clothing needed for given conditions, but rarely with enough attention given to detail. Improper clothing or the lack of special clothing can turn even a short distance into a life-threatening event. Two of the most common health problems that outdoor enthusiasts should know about and learn how to avoid are hypothermia and heat exhaustion, or heat stroke.

Hypothermia

Under normal circumstances, the body maintains a constant temperature of 98.6 degrees. As every cell in the body burns energy to function, they create heat. When used, organs or muscles get hotter. The body deals with this excess heat by spreading it out around the body through the blood to maintain a constant temperature. But what happens when the body is not creating enough heat?

Hypothermia occurs when body temperature drops below 95 degrees and continues to lose more heat than it can create. This condition, usually caused by exposure to cold, will have adverse effects on organs and systems including the brain, heart, and nervous system.

In cold weather navigation, anyone can suffer from hypothermia without realizing their condition. Hypothermia can set in without warning and if not treated, it can quickly lead to complete failure of your heart and respiratory system, and even death.

Too often, someone suffering from hypothermia may not even realize the condition has occurred because the beginning symptoms are mild and progress gradually. As the illness progresses, confused thinking will prevent self-awareness.

Avoiding Hypothermia

To minimize the risk of hypothermia, insulate your body from the effects of the cold. Heat loss through the head and neck can be minimized with the use of protective coverings like a hat and scarf. Protect your hands and fingers with gloves or mittens. Layer your clothing with loose-fitting material made of silk, wool, or polypropylene as the inner layers. These materials hold body heat better than others do. A shell layer (outer layer) should be a tightly woven, water-repellent material that will also provide wind protection.

Stay dry. Avoid overexertion whenever possible to reduce the effect of sweating. Change out of wet clothing as soon as possible. Wet clothing and cold temperatures will cause you to lose body heat more quickly. Pay special attention to gloves and shoes, as outermost extremities can be harder to keep warm and it can be much easier for snow and water to penetrate these areas.

Symptoms of Hypothermia

Mild hypothermia usually starts with simple shivers as temperatures drop. While not life threatening, shivers should be taken as a signal to begin watching over other symptoms that may follow, including dizziness, hunger, nausea, confusion, trouble speaking, poor coordination, fatigue, and increased heart rate. As the illness progresses and becomes moderate to severe, coordination turns to clumsiness and shivering will stop. Good decisions become harder to make due to confusion and lack of concern. Finally, slow breathing, a weak pulse, and very low energy will lead to loss of consciousness.

Hypothermia begins in cold weather conditions when your body heat is lost faster than it can be produced. Heat radiated from the body is lost due to improper clothing or exposed parts of the body. Exposure to cold water and wet clothes are also serious threats that can lead to hypothermia. Wind and wind chill factor are important to remember when preparing for movement across any terrain. Warm air at the surface of exposed skin will be taken away by any wind.

Treatment of Hypothermia

When hypothermia becomes evident while in the wilderness, give immediate attention to the affected person in your party and contact or signal for medical help. Until proper medical treatment can be provided, follow these guidelines for treatment.

Find shelter. Look for or construct a temporary shelter (Chapter 10) to protect against the cold and wind. If possible, find shelter that can retain heat or sustain a fire. Use care when moving or helping a person with hypothermia. In moderate to extreme cases, sudden or jarring movements can lead to cardiac arrest. Once moved to a protected location that is warm and dry, remove any wet clothing. Cut away clothing, if necessary, to prevent unneeded movement.

Create body heat. Use a blanket, sleeping bag, or other suitable item to keep the affected person's body warm and avoid direct contact with the ground. If no such object is available, improvise with a thick layer of leaves, small branches, or other foliage. Completely cover the person with layers of dry blankets, coats, or other clothing articles. To aid in warming a person's body, remove your own clothing and lie next to the person, making as much skin-to-skin contact as possible. Make sure both of your bodies are covered.

Hydrate. If the affected person is awake and able to swallow, warm beverages that are non-alcoholic and decaffeinated can be used to help warm the body. Never use hot water or other hot items to warm a person directly. Direct contact with extreme heat can damage the skin, or worse, can cause irregular heartbeats or even heart failure.

Warm the core. First aid warm compresses are essential to the prepper or survivalist. These plastic, fluid-filled bags will warm when squeezed, and can be applied to the neck, chest, or groin area. You can also use a makeshift compress, such as a plastic bottle filled with warm water and or a dry warm towel. Do not apply the warm compress to outer extremities of the body. Excessive heat applied to the arms and legs will force cold blood back to the heart, lungs, and brain, causing a drop in core body temperature.

Heat Exhaustion and Heat Stroke

In most parts of the world, even where temperatures are relatively mild during spring or fall, it's common to have a false sense of security in what is worn during a trip across country on foot. Unexpected changes in weather, unforeseen obstacles, or an unplanned overnight stay may have you wishing you had worn or brought along different clothing. During mid-summer when weather is relatively constant, the need for adequate clothing may become more obvious. When choosing clothing for a trek, you must account for distance, time, and terrain. While you may be comfortable when sitting and planning your course, forces immediately start generating heat in and around the body as soon as you actually start moving. Long journeys over tough terrain, or steep climbs during mild or hot days, can lead to heat exhaustion and even heat stroke.

When planning a day trip, you may want to start out on cold mornings by layering clothing. This can save time and make it easier to adjust by simply removing layers as the body and daytime temperatures begin to warm. Always adjust your clothing immediately when you feel your body warm; never wait until your body begins to sweat. Sweat is the natural result of the body attempting to cool itself, and while it is a good thing, the process takes away the body's moisture. Sweat can lead to dehydration, which in turn reduces your body's ability to sweat.

Along with dehydration, alcohol use will hinder your ability to sweat, affecting your body's attempts to maintain a proper core temperature. Overdressing and wearing clothes that don't allow your body sweat to evaporate easily may lead to heat exhaustion.

Avoiding Heat Exhaustion and Heat Stroke

When traveling to an area you're unfamiliar with, be careful of temperature changes and humidity. Higher temperatures or an early heat wave can make you more prone to heat-related illness, especially if you aren't used to heat. High humidity will also affect your body's ability to cool itself by slowing the process of sweat evaporation.

When planning a movement across land, consider the heat you may be exposed to and dress appropriately. Loose-fitting, lightweight, and light-colored clothing should be worn in hot conditions, as these will allow your body to cool itself through sweat evaporation. Wear a lightweight, wide-brimmed hat to protect your head and neck. Sunburned areas of the skin lose the ability to rid themselves of heat, making sunscreen a wise choice to carry in your pack.

A longer route offering more shade and easier navigation will reduce the possibility of heat exhaustion. Avoid hot spots when taking breaks and drink plenty of fluids. Temperatures may be a few degrees cooler when traveling alongside a stream or body of water, and the water will allow opportunities to cool the body if you feel overheated.

Caution: No one is immune to heat exhaustion, but the elderly are at greater risk due to illness, medications, and other factors associated with age. Children under the age of four are also at greater risk, as the body's ability to regulate temperature has not fully developed.

Pharmaceutical drugs such as heart medications, antihistamines, tranquilizers, and antipsychotics can all increase the risk of heat exhaustion. Illegal drugs like cocaine and amphetamines can also increase your body's core temperature.

Symptoms of Heat Exhaustion and Heat Stroke

When you are navigating rough terrain and experiencing prolonged periods of physical exertion, heat exhaustion signs and symptoms usually develop gradually. However, these symptoms can occur suddenly when preforming a task that demands more energy and/or is attempted in a shorter length of time. Higher temperatures will also add to the risk of heat exhaustion.

Heavy sweating or even cool, moist skin with goose bumps are both indicators of heat exhaustion. Faintness, a weak yet rapid pulse, dizziness, and fatigue are also common signs of heat exhaustion, along with muscle cramps, nausea, and headaches.

When heat exhaustion is not treated, heat stroke may follow. Heat stroke, more severe than heat exhaustion, occurs when the body's temperature rises to 104°F or higher. With heat stroke, the brain, heart, kidneys, and muscles can become damaged, leading to complications and death. Along with high body temperatures, the victim may show signs of odd mental behavior, vomiting, flushed skin, and racing heart rate. Heat stroke sufferers often stop sweating and have dry skin. When heat stroke is suspected, immediate medical attention must be provided.

Treatment of Heat Exhaustion and Heat Stroke

Heat exhaustion usually can be treated easily while out in the wilderness, but when heat exhaustion turns to heat stroke, immediate medical attention must be found. Untreated heat stroke can cause brain damage and damage to other internal organs that may lead to death.

If suffering from heat exhaustion, remove unneeded clothing first and find shade. Lie down on your back and keep your legs elevated above your heart level. Drink water or sports drinks, preferably chilled. Place wet towels or ice packs on your skin, if available. If you have access to a stream or body of water, cool yourself by taking a bath.

Using these treatment techniques, you'll usually notice a full recovery within one hour. If symptoms do not improve, consider seeking out professional medical attention.

WHEN YOU'RE LOST

It had been raining off and on all day, and not just occasional showers, but sporadic torrential downpours. Even with my rain gear, water seemed to find a way in and I was soaked from head to toe. I hadn't expected this when planning my route that morning. The sky was relatively clear, with only a few clouds and a moderate wind, but this had all changed by the time I hit my first checkpoint. The wind picked up and the clouds rolled in, completely covering the sky and turning the landscape into dark shadows. From checkpoint to checkpoint, not once did the clouds give way to the sun, making the entire day dark and gloomy.

I had planned this trip perfectly—well, almost. Whenever I'm preparing for any trip into the mountains, I do extensive planning. With up-to-date maps, I lay out my intended course. From beginning to end, I plot checkpoints, distance, terrain, time, weather, obstacles, and hazards. I try to consider all the possibilities of what could happen, like unavoidable detours or an injury, and I prepare for these as well. Under normal circumstances, I would also verify the contents of my backpack with my written checklist, developed over the years to include the most important essentials that I always carry.

However, on this particular trip I did not use my checklist. I had misplaced my list, but having planned countless similar trips, I was not concerned that memory would fail me. I was wrong. Without extra batteries for my GPS device, it became just added weight after the first day. I was not too concerned; many times, I'd been unable to receive a signal anyway, and I always carry my compass.

I knew that I had just missed my last checkpoint, but it couldn't have been by much, so I pushed on. My next checkpoint was close and even though visibility was poor, I was sure I would hit my mark. Certain of this, and knowing my final destination was just beyond, I continued. I picked up the pace, knowing I had only an hour or so to reach my planned camp before that gray day turned to night.

Soon, I'd missed both of my last checkpoints and I was unable to see landmarks at all. If I'd wanted to continue, I would have been navigating in the rain at night, by dead reckoning alone, on a course I was no longer sure of. Continuing at that point could only make matters worse. Instead, I remained calm, sat below a nearby tree that offered a little protection from the rain, and faced the humiliation of being lost as I waited for morning to bring new light.

The following morning found me in a better mood. Though I got no sleep the night before, I did manage to get a fire started. With the fire, I was able to stay warm, and as the rain subsided, I had somewhat dried out my clothing. It was still overcast but there was no rain, and I had plenty of light to inspect my surroundings. Not far from my current location was a ridge that looked as if it could provide a good vantage point to better survey the area. After a quick meal, I left my campsite and hiked the 20 minutes it took to reach the top of the ridge.

From my new vantage point, I was able to identify several outlying objects and find these same landmarks on my map.

Using resection, I was able to take compass bearings to three different objects and transfer them to my map, pinpointing my exact location. I was only off course by approximately 200 yards, but had I continued on the night before, it could have been much worse.

Thinking back now, I had two clear options that could have left me in better spirits. Option number one would have been to backtrack to my last confirmed checkpoint after realizing I missed the next checkpoint before continuing on. Option two, and probably the best option considering it had been late in the day, would have been to backtrack to my last confirmed checkpoint, build a shelter and fire, and camp there for the night.

Knowing When You Are Lost

Seasoned adventurers know they are not immune to getting lost. Even with a map and compass, many of the most experienced in land navigation have found themselves wondering exactly where they were. Whether due to an outdated map, faulty equipment, or changes in terrain and landmarks, countless scenarios can all lead to doubt and errors in navigation. The first step in recovery from being lost in the wilderness is accepting the possibility that it has happened. Then you can take the necessary steps to fix the problem.

Fear and Panic

When you find yourself with even the slightest doubt as to where you are or where you should go, you are lost. Immediately finding or recognizing a landmark does not change the fact that for a moment, you were lost. It's during this moment of realization that fear, however slight, begins to grow in the back of your mind.

Both fear and panic will lead to hasty and often wrong decisions and must be dealt with before making your next steps. Stop whatever it is you're doing, relax, and stay calm. Take the time to sit and think about where you're going, where you have been, and the steps taken leading up to this point. Picture in your mind the landscape, terrain, or other features and landmarks seen along the way. Study your current surroundings, the horizon, the clouds in the sky, and even the time of day. This time spent on close examination of your situation will keep fear and panic at bay and may give you clues as to your position.

A large pack on your shoulders will never carry as much or be as useful as a clear head. However, when planning a trip into the wilderness, a wise person will also plan on getting lost and prepare for the event. Fishing line and a few hooks, waterproof matches or lighters, a map, a compass, some concentrated food, and a good knife may save you a lot of grief.

A thinking person is never lost for long. Often, surviving the first night in the wilderness will bring a clear head the next morning with new insight regarding your location. With a relaxed mind, you'll realize that you can eat the same wild food animals eat and that you won't die of hunger as quickly as you will die of thirst. A calm and clear head will also tell you when it's time to stay put or when it's time to move on to some definite objective; you'll know how to avoid becoming totally exhausted or further lost. Find strength in the knowledge that someone will be looking for you; with this, the experience of being lost becomes easier to deal with.

Make a Decision

When you're lost, there are only two options: stay put, or continue on. Both plans have their advantages and disadvantages. The decision you make could be the difference between life and death.

Before making a decision, take inventory of what you have on hand, giving particular attention to food, water, and shelter. With water and food at the top of the list, how long can you survive after your supplies run out? Unless you're fortunate enough to have a resource for water nearby, you have three days to be found once your supply of water runs out.

Use the following list of questions as guideline in making your decision:

- How long will my current supply of food and water last?

- What effects will weather conditions have on me if I should stay or move?

- Do I have the resources at hand to construct a temporary shelter?

- Can I signal for help using smoke, mirrors, phone, radio, or other means?

- When will I be missed by friends or loved ones, and how long will it take them or others to start searching?

Staying Put

So here you sit. You've assessed the situation, taken inventory of the supplies you have on hand, considered the possibility of being found, and compared this to the alternative of moving on. You know there is a chance that if you keep moving, you may find a landmark you recognize—a road perhaps, or a river—but you also realize you may only become increasingly lost while using up what little supplies you have. So you decide to stay and wait for help.

Now that the decision has been made and you know you'll be spending an unexpected night in the wilderness, you need to start planning. Darkness may be approaching, or it may be several hours away. In either case, unless you're experiencing a warm summer night with perfect conditions, shelter must take priority over all else. You must ensure that you'll be protected from the elements.

Find the best suitable area at your current location to make camp. Use your surroundings, keeping in mind that you want to make it as easy as possible to be found while staying as comfortable as possible. Look for the closest area near you that offers both protection from the elements and the best opportunities to be found and to signal others of your location. Once steps have been made to secure a shelter, you can spend time on other essential actions.

Signaling for Help

When lost or even hurt in a survival situation, time may not be on your side. If not properly prepared, or if you're dealing with unfavorable conditions, survival may be short lived. Even when others notice your absence or late arrival, they have to find you before they can rescue you.

There are many methods of alerting people to your location, including electronic devices. However, because of the possibility of failure, damage, or dead batteries, take the time to focus more on using simple items. Learn and practice the following techniques to signal for help.

There are several ways to signal for help. Before you choose a method, consider your location: can you be seen or heard from where you are? The best location for signaling is a large, flat elevated point that is clear of obstruction and can be seen from the greatest distance possible.

Remember the rule of three. When it comes to signals, whether gunshots, smoke signals, a whistle, signal fires, or most other means used, a group of three is commonly recognized as an emergency distress signal.

Whistles

The whistle is the simplest of audio devices that can be used when in distress. The most common universal distress signal with a whistle is three short blasts. While range is limited, whistling will make it easier for those looking for you as they get closer to your location. While you may have other means of signaling at your disposal, it's advised that you use the whistle periodically. You may not see them, but searchers may start to hear you and need additional whistles to pinpoint your location. If you're traveling with others, make sure that all recognize the distress signal or other signals you may implement.

Choose a whistle that can be easily attached to your pack, belt loop, or other item of clothing. A one-piece whistle that does not require a pea is the best choice. These are usually less susceptible to damage and freezing conditions. I would also recommend a bright color so you can easily find it if dropped or misplaced.

Mirrors

A mirror may be the best way to visually create signals when you have the sun to work with. The sun's reflection from even a small mirror can be seen for miles on a clear day. A properly directed flash of light can be seen by aircraft, vehicles, or other people, catching their attention. Some mirrors are equipped with a sighting lens to help direct your signals. If your mirror does not have this feature, hold the mirror under your eye, and place the reflected beam of light onto the tip of an outstretched finger. While keeping the reflected light on the finger, move the finger and mirror together until the finger is on your target. Slowly move the mirror up and down, right to left. This will move the beam of light across your target.

If you don't have a mirror, other metallic items in your possession may fill the need. Try polishing a belt buckle, a canteen or cup, a large silver coin, or another object that will reflect the sun's light. As with all survival equipment, practice with what you have.

Fire and Smoke

Nothing beats a fire for getting the attention of anyone within visible range, especially at night. During the day, smoke from a fire can be seen for many miles. Be careful in selecting your location. As with any distress signal, find the nearest location with an open area that can be seen from the greatest distance and multiple directions. A signal from the side of a ridge or mountain generally can only be seen on that side. At the same time, you must consider your surroundings and look out for nearby flammable objects. A clearing devoid of trees or near a stream or river (which will act as a firebreak) will help you keep a signal fire under control when a larger fire is used or needed. Take caution not to endanger yourself or others when using fire.

When using fire to signal for help, also take note of the wind and the effect it will have on the fire. A light wind of up to 10 miles an hour may not be an issue in keeping a fire under control. However, stronger winds will make both the fire and the smoke harder to control and are much more dangerous.

During daylight hours, smoke is much easier to see than the fire itself. Once you're confident you have a hot bed of coals, add "green" materials, like live plants, leaves, or pine needles. Even a small fire with a good bed of hot coals can produce a large amount of smoke. Plant material that has not completely dried out, such as leaves, small bushes, or pinecones, will still burn and provide a greater amount of smoke than dry limbs or branches. Most materials you burn in the wild will produce a white or gray smoke and can be harder to see on cloudy days. Petroleum-based products, such as a few ounces of motor oil, brake fluid, or pieces of plastic, will produce a black smoke.

When using fire to signal at night, use only dry materials, if possible. Be sure you have enough material stacked and ready beforehand to keep your fire burning. Don't be caught having to leave your fire unattended to gather more wood, especially at night. Smoke is not always easily seen at night, but the light a fire emits is, and a larger fire will be easier seen from greater distances. If enough material is available and your area is large enough, build three fires in a straight row, 50 to 75 feet apart. This pattern is identified by most search-and-rescue teams as a distress signal. However, unless you have help in maintaining three fires, it may be safer to concentrate on building and using only one signal fire. Don't build a fire larger than you can control. Remove materials from the immediate surrounding area that may easily cause a fire to spread.

Using an isolated tree as a giant torch is a great way to attract attention. Trees producing a lot of sap or pitch are generally easy to set afire, even when they are green. If the lower limbs and branches are close enough to the ground, build a large enough fire around the base of the tree that the flames flare up and ignite the foliage. If needed, place dry twigs, branches, and other material into the lower branches, and set this material on fire. Before the tree has completely burned, cut and add more small green trees or bushes to the fire.

When the ground is covered in snow, scrape away the snow from the area where you intend to build a fire, or build a platform of limbs or small logs on which to build the fire.

For more on fire-making skills, see Chapter 12.

Improvise

Using your imagination and the natural materials that surround you to signal can get you found. Tree branches, limbs, small logs, bushes, or even rocks can be used to spell out a message or symbols on the ground. Use materials that stand out against the ground you're placing them on. Bright-colored clothing placed in an open area may attract attention. Large geometric patterns will more likely attract attention.

When there is snow, pack down the snow to form the message or symbol and fill the packed area with contrasting leaves, brush, or other darker materials. If there is little snow, scrape the snow away to expose the darker ground beneath to form your message.

Many of the techniques described are most suited to signal aircraft, but when placed on the side of a ridge or mountain, some of these methods may still be seen by those on the ground. In taking this approach, try to use the side of the ridge or mountain that is most likely to be seen.

Lights or flags can be used to send an SOS. Internationally recognized, an SOS is made up of three dots, three dashes, and three dots. This can be communicated with the use of a flashlight by interrupting the beam of light with your hand or other object. Many flashlights have a button to facilitate signaling. A flag can also be used to signal an SOS. When using flags, hold flags on the left side of your body for dashes and on the right side for dots.

Continuing On

Sometimes, the best choice to make when lost is to keep moving. Before you begin your move, look for an elevated area nearby, like a ridge or large hill, climb to the top, and look around for any recognizable landmark. Consider your immediate position and ask yourself these questions:

- If I continue in this direction, will I become even harder to find?

- Do I try to backtrack to terrain, a landmark, or a trail that I will recognize?

- Do I know which direction to travel to find the closest populated area?

Use your map and compass if these items are still available. You already know the general direction you took to get to where you are. If in getting there you traveled northwest, use your compass to head back in a southeast direction. While traveling, look for landmarks and other signs that you may recognize or find on your map. If you find a landmark and can identify it on your map, try to find another, which will allow you to do a resection and pinpoint your exact location. Or, you can continue on to that landmark while searching for another landmark.

As a last resort, especially if you're in higher elevations or in the mountains with no idea which direction to take, your first choice should be down. Follow drainage, streams, or a river, if possible. This could make for hard travel, but will often lead to a trail or a road.

Trail Markers

Let people know where you have been and where you're going. Two great tools to keep in your backpack at all times are brightly colored survey tape or flash tape and a permanent ink marker. With these tools, you can easily tear off pieces to mark trails you have taken and even leave messages on the tape. Flash tape, used by gardeners to scare off birds, is highly reflective and will act like a mirror to reflect the sun's light and catch the attention of anyone looking in its direction.

Small logs, branches, or rocks can also be used to alert searchers or others in your party of the direction you have taken. Make these markers as large as possible and place in areas where they will most likely be noticed.

10

FINDING SHELTER

If you planned properly before your trip into unfamiliar surroundings, someone knows where you are, or at least has a general idea as to your location. If you're lost, stay where you are or as close to that position as possible and find a suitable spot that will provide you with shelter. Along with providing protection from the elements, a shelter will provide visibility. Have your shelter in an area that can be easily seen, or get as close as possible to such an area. You need to be able to signal and see others that may be in the area, and you need to be seen by those that may be searching for you. Remember: don't make it any harder to be found by traveling farther off course than you need to.

A shelter only needs to be large enough to protect you from the elements: sun, rain, snow, and various temperatures. In colder climates, smaller shelters are better to help contain body heat. Not only will a shelter provide you with protection, it will give you a more positive outlook on your situation and increase your will to live.

Countless shelters can be constructed quickly and easily for protection from the elements with minimal materials and tools. The following are a few of the most practical and easiest to build. All of these shelters can be expanded upon, depending on your needs and the materials you have at hand. Other than your situation and current conditions, limitations are governed only by your imagination.

Site Selection

When you realize you're in a survival situation and shelter is a priority, start looking for shelter or the materials you'll need right away. The site you select must contain the materials to build a suitable shelter. The site must also be level and large enough to sit and lie down in comfortably. Consider the following before you begin:

- Will the planned site give you any protection from animals, insects, poisonous snakes, or plants?

- Will you be able to signal for help?

- Do you have the tools, or can you improvise and make the tools you need to construct the shelter?

- Do you have the materials at hand to make the type of shelter you want?

- How much effort is required?

- Do you have the time to build the shelter you have in mind?

Your environment must also be evaluated. Take special considerations depending on the season. What may be an ideal site in winter may not be practical in summer. In winter or cold months, you'll need protection from the low temperatures and wind. During these same months, you'll also need the material to build and feed a fire, as well as a source for water. During the summer months, you'll still need water, but now you may be overwhelmed with insects, snakes, and other animals.

Other problems that could arise in selecting your site may include flash flood areas in foothills, avalanches or rockslides in mountainous terrain, and the various dangers of a site located too close to a stream or body of water.

Field and Forest Shelters

For any given situation, you can construct several types of shelters if you know how to make them and what materials you'll need. Just a little bit of thought and imagination will go a long way. On the next family outing or camping trip, take the time to practice building different shelters with the materials you find around you.

Lean-to with firewall

Poncho Lean-To

In navigation, the equipment you carry will keep you safe and has to be of good quality and functional. This holds true for the poncho. A quality poncho is a great piece of equipment with many other uses besides keeping you warm and dry. The poncho can come in many different styles and sizes. It should be made of a ripstop nylon, have a drawstring hood, have double-sided snaps for closing or attaching to another poncho, and have grommets to tie to other objects.

I usually carry a poncho when in the wilderness or hiking across country, even in the best of weather. The poncho is lightweight and can be folded to a small size for storage in a pack. Besides protection from weather, a quality poncho can be used to collect water, carry or drag different items, create smoke signals, and act as a wind block. At night, a poncho can be filled with leaves, pine needles, or other foliage, and then be snapped shut to make a comfortable bed. It can also be used as a blanket, mattress, pillow, or even hammock. A poncho can also be cut into strips and used as cordage or bandage material. I've even used a poncho to dam up a small stream, giving myself a small pond to bath in.

For an easy and effective shelter that requires little time, minimal effort, and few materials, a poncho is a great resource. Only a few items are required to construct the poncho lean-to or tent. You'll need 3 or more feet of support rope or paracord; three to six stakes, each approximately 1 foot in length; two trees or two poles set in the ground vertically, 6 to 10 feet apart; drip sticks or string; and a poncho. Keep wind direction in mind when selecting the trees. Make sure that the back of your lean-to or tent will be facing the wind.

1. Fold and secure the poncho's hood using the drawstring.

2. Cut your support rope or paracord in half. Tie one half of the rope to the corner grommet on one long side of the poncho.

3. Tie the other half of the rope to the other corner grommet on the same side.

4. At about waist height, tie the other ends of these two ropes to the trees or poles.

5. Spread out the poncho and anchor it to the ground by driving the stakes through the remaining corner grommets and those grommets along that edge that meets the ground.

6. Tie a drip stick or string approximately 6 inches long to each rope, about 1 inch from the grommet. Tie additional strings to each grommet along the top edge of the poncho. Water will run down these drip sticks and strings without dripping into the shelter.

Additional support for an extended stay or in case of rain can be made by attaching another length of paracord to the poncho hood with the other end tied to an overhanging branch. You can also place a stick upright in the center of the poncho, but this would limit space for movement within the shelter. Your pack, brush, or other suitable materials can be placed along the sides to create additional protection. Cover the ground inside the shelter with leaves, branches, or other foliage to keep your body from direct contact with the ground. While resting, you can transfer as much as 80 percent of your body heat to the ground when making direct contact.

A poncho tent can also be constructed in almost the same manner, giving you protection from the elements on two sides. However, a tent set-up will leave you with less space inside the shelter. In constructing the tent, one end of each support rope would be tied to the poncho's center grommet on each side, and the other ends would be tied tightly to each tree or pole at about knee height. You would then pull one side of the poncho tight and secure it to the ground by pushing the stakes into the ground through the grommets. Once one side has been secured, repeat this procedure on the other side.

If additional support is needed, you can use the same technique as in the lean-to to secure a line to the poncho's hood. You can also build an A-frame set outside, over the center of the tent. Using two 4- or 5-foot poles, form an A-frame over the middle of the tent, tying the poncho's hood drawstring to the top of the A.

Field Lean-To

When in the woods, you'll probably have enough natural materials on hand to construct a lean-to without using your poncho. A field lean-to is a great choice and can be constructed without the use of any tools, although an ax or a sharp knife will make the job easier. It requires a little more time to build, but the size of the field lean-to will not be as limited as it would be if using a poncho.

As with the poncho lean-to, the field lean-to requires two trees or two poles to hold up your horizontal support. The horizontal support should be 6 to 8 feet long with a diameter large enough to support the weight of the leaves, pine needles, grass, and other materials you use for covering. You'll also need five to eight poles, each 10 to 12 feet long and approximately 2 inches in diameter; cordage or vines to secure the horizontal support and poles where needed; and other smaller poles, vines, or saplings to crisscross the beams.

1. Using available cordage, secure the horizontal pole to the two trees at waist or chest height. Sometimes an existing tree branch is available to help in this support.

2. If there are no trees or only one tree at your location, create a vertical support by making a tripod, or make a biped using Y-shaped sticks.

3. At evenly spaced intervals, lean each of your beams along one side of your horizontal support. Secure with

cordage if available. Remember to keep the backside of the lean-to against the wind.

4. Crisscross saplings, vines, or other small-diameter poles on the beams.

5. Once the framework is complete, you can cover with brush, leaves, pine needles, or grass, starting at the bottom and working your way up. Overlap the material like shingling.

To prevent cold weather or to minimize wind, you can make any lean-to much more comfortable with the use of a fire reflector wall.

At a safe distance but close to the open side of your lean-to, drive 4- to 5-foot-long stakes into the ground to form a rectangle with an area of approximately 1 foot by 4 feet, with the 4-foot side facing the lean-to. This will not only provide the maximum amount of heat reflected by the fire, but will also act as a wind break. Stack two rows of green logs 4 to 5 feet long within the stakes, filling the space between the two rows of logs with dirt. The dirt will strengthen the wall and will help reflect the heat from the fire. Secure the tops of the stakes to each other using cordage or rope so the logs and dirt remain in place. Build your fire 12 to 18 inches away from the firewall so that the heat generated reflects back to your shelter. With a little more effort and a few more materials, you can now easily build a drying rack. Cut a few poles, their length depending on the distance between the horizontal support pole of the lean-to and the firewall. Lay one end of each poll across the horizontal support pole and the other end across the top of the firewall. You can now tie smaller sticks across these poles, giving you a place to dry clothes, meat, or fish.

Debris Hut

If a fast, easy shelter is required, a debris hut is one of the best. A common debris hut has no room for upright movement but provides warmth and protection from the elements.

1. Construct a tripod by securing the end of one long ridgepole on a base that is 4 to 5 feet high. This base can be a tree stump, a low-hanging branch with a large diameter, a boulder, or another solid object. You could also build a tripod with two short stakes and the ridgepole if a suitable base isn't available.

2. Create a wedge-shaped frame by propping large sticks along the entire length of both sides of the ridgepole. Make sure that the space provided between the large sticks or ribbings on both sides is large enough to accommodate a person and steep enough to allow rain to shed.

3. Once the framework is complete, crisscross finer sticks and brush along the ribbing. Keep in mind that these will become the latticework that will keep the insulating material (pine needles, grass, leaves, etc.) from falling through into the sleeping area.

4. Now, add your debris on top of the hut until the material is at least 3 feet thick, if possible. The thicker, the better. Use light and dry materials.

5. After the debris has been added, cover it with shingling material, like bark or branches, to keep the insulating material in place and prevent it from blowing away in stormy conditions.

6. Avoid body heat transfer and further protect yourself from the cold by adding a 12-inch layer of insulating material to the floor of the hut.

7. As a final step in construction, pile insulating material in front of the opening that can be dragged toward you to close the entrance once inside, or build a door.

Debris hut

Snow Shelters

Tree-Pit Shelter

Unlike some fair-weather shelters, most snow shelters will require some type of tool to move snow or cut blocks of snow. However, the simplest of snow shelters can be constructed without the use of any tool, requiring only your hands, a shovel, or some other makeshift tool for digging.

When shelter becomes a necessity in snowy winter weather, a tree-pit shelter may be the simplest option to give you protection. As most trees are suitable to work with, a tree-pit shelter is simple and easy to build. Using a tree with branches to provide some overhead cover will work best. They will protect you from the wind and keep you warm.

1. Dig out the snow around the base of the tree until you reach a desired diameter and depth, or until you reach the ground.

2. Pack the snow on the inside of the hole for support. Add more around the top of the hole if more height is required and pack this snow.

3. Cover the bottom of the hole with evergreen boughs, small limbs, pine needles, or whatever else is available for insulation. Use bigger limbs, bushy branches, or boughs to cover the top of the hole.

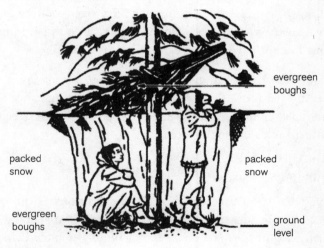

evergreen boughs

packed snow

packed snow

evergreen boughs

ground level

Tree-pit snow shelter

Snow Cave

If you have the time, skills, and adequate conditions, a snow cave shelter is the most effective shelter because of its insulating properties. If conditions are good, even a novice can get satisfactory results on the first try, but plan on getting wet and spending two to three hours on construction.

To build a snow cave, you must first locate a snowdrift 8 feet wide or more in which to dig. The ceiling and walls should be at least one 1 thick and the interior must have a ventilation shaft to the outside. If your drift isn't quite large enough, you can improvise by piling additional snow where needed before digging out the cave. While digging a cave into the side of the drift, you must keep the roof arched. This will support the structure and allow melted snow to run down the sides.

Your sleeping spot should be located away from the door and on a platform slightly higher than the rest of the floor. Separate the platform from the wall by digging a small channel between the wall and the platform. The raised platform and channel will keep you and your equipment dry from melting snow. This construction is especially important if you plan to build a small fire or have other means to heat the interior.

Be sure the roof is high enough that you can sit up on the sleeping platform. Create a door or block the entrance with material at hand and use the lower area away from the sleeping platform as your cooking area.

Quinzhee

If you have the time and the right conditions, a quinzhee shelter can be just as effective as a cave shelter in keeping you warm. A quinzhee shelter does not require a snowdrift or a tree; only level ground, a lot of snow, and a lot of work.

1. Start by finding a suitable, level area 6 to 10 feet in diameter. An area with a depression in the ground would be a benefit.

2. Pile snow in the location selected, creating a mound or dome at least $4\frac{1}{2}$ to 6 feet high and 6 to 10 feet wide.

3. Once you have created the mound, let it set for 30 to 60 minutes, allowing it to settle and consolidate. If available, force sticks 12 to 14 inches deep into the mound. These sticks will act as a guide to maintaining a uniform thickness and arch in the roof as you remove snow from inside.

4. Select a spot for your entrance with consideration of wind. A downhill location will allow cold air to drift out of the shelter. At ground level, start digging an entrance that is only large enough to crawl through.

5. Once inside the mound, start excavating upward in arcs to create a dome within. The sticks that were placed into the dome outside will tell you where to stop digging. Continue digging out the snow from the top down and remove it from inside the shelter as you go.

6. As you get closer to the outside wall, scrape only 2 to 3 inches at a time until you reach the sticks you placed. Maintaining the dome shape and a wall thickness of at least 1 foot will give you a shelter with the strength it requires and excellent insulation.

As with the snow cave, creating a sleeping platform will help to keep you dry. Use your backpack, raincoat, brush, or other available materials to block the entrance once inside.

Igloo

For the ultimate protection in winter conditions, nothing can outperform the igloo. A well-constructed igloo will not only keep you warm and protect you from the wind; it's also more permanent and resilient. The well-constructed igloo can have an inner temperature ranging from 19°F to 61°F with an outside temperature as low as -49°F. While an igloo can outperform a snow cave or quinzhee shelter, it's also the hardest to build correctly.

Building an igloo takes practice and a large knife or saw. Even with the skill required to construct an igloo, it can take one person over four hours to build. If immediate shelter is required and you have no hands-on experience in building an igloo, other options should be considered.

In a survival situation, an igloo can be built into the side of a slope, saving time and energy. By building your igloo into the side of a hill or drift, you can cut down on the surface area of the dome. Less surface area means fewer blocks of snow and less work. To simplify the explanation, we will assume you're on flat level ground.

1. Before you begin construction, find a suitable area of level ground that is at least 6 feet in diameter. The snow on the ground must be at least 2 feet deep and hard packed, containing no layers of soft snow. This can be checked by using a long stick and poking it into the ground at several locations to check its consistency. The snow should have a firm, uniform, hard-packed resistance throughout the area you plan to build. The bricks you'll be using to construct the igloo will come from within this area and additional blocks, if needed, will come from outside your planned igloo.

2. Mark the outline of the outer wall of the igloo using the heel of your boot or a stick, making as perfect a circle as possible. This can be easily done by driving a stick into the snow at the center of where the igloo will be. Tie a piece of string or rope measuring half the diameter of the igloo to the stick. While holding the other end of the string taut, walk around the stick using your heel

to scuff the outer perimeter. Keep it simple; never build an igloo larger than 10 feet in diameter. The accuracy required to build an igloo this size is difficult to achieve even with special tools.

3. Section the hard-packed snow inside your circle into equally sized rectangular blocks. The blocks may vary depending on the size of your igloo, but traditionally they are 3 feet long, 15 inches high, and 8 inches thick.

4. Cut the blocks to the size you require and use your cutting tool to wiggle and loosen stubborn blocks free. As you cut the blocks, arrange them around the perimeter of your igloo to create the first layer of your dome. Use your knife, machete, or saw to smooth the surfaces of the blocks and fill any cracks or holes with snow.

5. Cut a gradual slope in the first row of blocks. This slope should include $\frac{1}{3}$ to as much as half the circumference of the igloo's first row. This incline will allow the bricks to be stacked in a vertical spiral, providing a solid fit. With your cutting tool, bevel the top of this row of blocks so that the next row of blocks will be leaning slightly toward the center of your igloo. Each new row should be started from the sloping end of the previous row with the top edge beveled inward.

6. The final block, or cap block, can be tricky to get right. Turn your last block on end and gently work it through the top hole to set it in place. Use your knife or cutting tool to shape it for a snug fit. Once the top is in place, fill all cracks and holes with loose snow.

7. With the igloo frame completed, it's time to cut the door for your entrance. Crouching or on your knees, cut your doorway from the bottom to about eye level. Make it

wide enough for you to crawl through. You can save this block by pulling it into the igloo and using it as a crawl space for your entrance. Clear away snow as needed from outside your entranceway in an upward slope.

8. Cut the block you removed from the entrance in half. Outside the entrance, lean the two halves together so they hold each other up, creating an A-shaped crawl space entrance. Make sure the edges of this crawl space you created are snug against the igloo entrance.

9. Outside the igloo, fill in all cracks and holes with loose snow. Cut small crescent shapes in the top or around the sides to prevent the buildup of CO_2.

Besides acting as an exceptional insulator, the shape of the igloo will resist the wind. An igloo can be warm with just body heat or with a small, carefully tended fire. Using candles can also warm an igloo several degrees. The inside wall may melt slightly, but will refreeze to create an ice layer when the heat is removed. This will make the igloo stronger.

Other Snow Shelters

As with any type of shelter, snow shelters can be modified, adjusted, or tweaked to fit your needs. Many of the earlier shelters described can be used in conjunction with snow. For example, the poncho lean-to, the field lean-to, and the debris hut can all be used as the foundation for a snow shelter when the materials are available. Once constructed, modify these shelters by using the snow to reinforce or cover the structure, allowing for the additional weight of snow in the framework.

A survival shelter can be made simple with a clear mind, a little time, and the imagination to use the resources at hand.

Desert Shelters

Many desert environments offer few resources to aid in building a shelter. Take a moment to consider the time, effort, and material needed to make a shelter. If you have a poncho, canvas, extra clothing, or other materials, use them along with available terrain features such as rock outcroppings, depressions in the terrain, mounds of sand, or small sand dunes.

Outcroppings

If you have a rock outcropping and a poncho or similar material, anchor one end of the material to the outcropping. Extend the other end and anchor it to provide the best shade possible. Make use of any nearby bushes, trees, or the limbs of a tree to act as additional covering for shade.

Sandy Areas

In sandy areas when no outcropping is available, build or use a mound of sand to act as one side of the shelter. Anchor one end of your material to the top of the mound using sand, rocks, or other weights. Extend the other end and anchor it to the ground to provide the best shade possible. As before, make use of any other available materials you may have near you to provide additional shade.

If you have enough material on hand for the roof of your shelter, fold it in half to create an air pocket between the two layers. Airspace of at least 12 to 16 inches between the two layers above your shelter will reduce the temperature by several degrees.

Belowground

While it may take more time and energy to construct, a belowground shelter can reduce the temperature by as much as 30°F to 40°F. Sweat and dehydration become an important factor in deserts and consideration should be given to building the shelter before the heat of the day or before it is late at night.

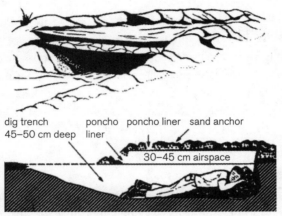

dig trench   poncho   poncho liner   sand anchor
45–50 cm deep   liner

30–45 cm airspace

Belowground shelter

An ideal location for a belowground shelter would be an existing low spot or depression.

1. If required, dig out a trench 1 ½ to 2 ½ feet deep, long and wide enough for you to lie down in comfortably.

2. Pile the sand you take from the trench and form a mound around three sides.

3. Cover the trench with your material and hold it in place using sand, rocks, or other material.

4. Dig more sand out of the open end of trench, if needed, making for easy entrance.

5. For maximum protection, use two layers of covering with air space in between. A white or light-colored outer covering will also reflect more heat; the inner layer should be a darker color.

Natural Shelters

Before taking on the task of building a shelter, check your surroundings. Nature may have provided you with the best of shelters that may be ready to go or require very little modifications. Caves, rock outcroppings, large trees, fallen trees, or ground depressions may be suitable to provide shelter.

In selecting a natural shelter, be aware of ticks, ants, poisonous snakes, or other insects and animals that can make your situation more unpleasant. Avoid lower ground where heavy, cold air will collect. Low ground, ravines, narrow valleys, or dry creek beds can also lead to wet conditions and should be avoided. Check your immediate area for other potential hazards like loose rocks, dead limbs, or other natural growth that could fall on your shelter. In winter during snowfall, or as temperatures warm, snow collected on the branches of trees can also be a hazard for that shelter underneath.

11

OBTAINING WATER

The weekend had arrived, and none too soon. The next day would be Sunday, one week into what I had planned to be a two-week camp-out. While I had a few menial tasks to preform each day, I was glad to have had the foresight to bring along a deck of cards and a book to read. I had also taken the time to make myself a pair of snowshoes using only some branches from a nearby tree and a section of rope I'd unbraided. After being snowed in for a week, I was looking forward to making the hike back to the point where I'd been dropped off before the storm.

Other than the first snow, which remained with the colder temperatures, the weather had been good. Needing very little wood to keep such a small cabin warm, I had no concerns of running out. I had a fire only in the evenings and early morning as I planned another day.

Before the snowfall, water was not a concern for me, as Todd Lake was only a mile away. I had not made the hike back to the lake since the snow. I had a water supply on hand that had since run out, but now I had plenty of snow. It was bit of a blessing not having to make the hike for water, but even more of a blessing not having to carry it back. I simply scooped up a bucket of snow and set it inside the cabin, where after a few hours I would have fresh water.

What if the circumstances had been different? What if there was no Todd Lake or an abundance of snow? Where and how would I get the water I needed to survive more than three days in any environment?

When lost and in a survival situation, water is at the top of the list as an urgent need, along with shelter. Over 75 percent of your body is made up of fluids. These fluids are constantly being lost through heat, cold, stress, exertion, and evaporation, even when you're sitting still. Three days is the standard for surviving without water, and on hot days where you lose moisture rapidly through perspiration, the time could be less. Even on cold days, the body requires a minimum of 2 liters, or ½ gallon, of water each day to function properly.

Many of the following ways to procure water can be found in the *U.S. Army Survival Manual FM 21-76*. There are several that I personally have not tried, and there are a few that may appear to require a lot of time and effort for very little water. However, when it comes to a survival situation, a small amount of water can mean the difference between life and death. To that end, all are worth understanding and being familiar with.

Sources for Water

Caution: Always purify water before drinking. See techniques for purifying water further on.

When water isn't visible, it may be found hiding in nature in many different places. Some of these resources are easily visible when you know what to look for, while others are better hidden and require observation. However, all are accessible with a little know-how and ingenuity.

Dew is a common source for water that may be right at your feet. It can be found almost anywhere, given the right conditions. Dew is formed when thin objects cool, radiate their heat, and cause moisture in the cooler air around them to condensate on the object. This process happens when outside temperatures are coolest, during evenings and mornings.

Heavy dew on grass can be collected by wrapping an absorbent cloth or tufts of fine grass to your ankles and slowly walking through the dew-covered grass. As the cloth or grass tufts absorb the dew, periodically stop and wring the water into a container. Natives in Australia use this method to collect as much as a liter of water every hour. Other resources claimed you could collect as much as 4 liters in one hour. Dew can also be found on metal surfaces and captured by using an absorbent material that can be wrung out.

Areas with lush green plants or an abundance of vegetation may be an indicator of nearby water. Dig a hole in the ground near these plants to look for signs of moist dirt. If you notice darker, moister dirt, digging a little further may cause water to start seeping into the hole you created.

Rock crevices, hollows, or crotches in trees may contain water that can be removed with a makeshift cup, a straw used for siphoning, or an absorbent cloth. In dry, acrid areas, bird droppings around a crack in the rocks may indicate water. Bees or ants going into a hole of a tree may be pointing you to a source of water. Shaded areas in canyons and valleys during the heat of the day may also have hidden water. Moisture from earlier snowfalls or rainfalls are more likely to be retained in these shaded areas, even months after a major downpour. Look for depressions in dry streams or riverbeds. Usually found at a bend, along an outside edge, or where water fell from one level to another, these depressions may contain water just under the surface.

Plants and Trees

A few different plants and trees contain water and it may be that you have one or more of these in your area.

A banana or plantain tree can be cut down to procure water. Cut down the tree about a foot above the ground, leaving you a stump. Scoop the top of the stump into the shape of a bowl. The stump will begin to fill quickly with the water from its roots. Remove and discard water from the first three or four times the bowl fills, as this water will be bitter. The following water will be palatable. This technique will supply you with water for several days. Cover the stump when it's not in use to avoid contamination from insects or animals.

Tropical vines can also be a source for water. Cut a notch into the vine as high as possible, then, with a container ready, cut the vine close to the ground. Use your container to catch the liquid, or hold the vine to your mouth to drink.

Caution: Do not drink the liquid if it is sticky, milky, or bitter tasting.

If you're fortunate enough to have coconut trees near you, the green, unripe coconuts are a good source for quenching your thirst. But beware of the mature coconuts, which contain oil that will act as a laxative. This mature coconut milk can still be used to ward off dehydration, but in moderation only.

In the American tropics, the branches of large trees support air plants. Air plants have thick-growing leaves that overlap, making a good collector of rainwater. However, in collecting the rainwater, you'll need to strain the water through a cloth to remove insects and other debris.

Other trees that contain water include palms, like coconut, sugar, buri, and nips. By bruising or cutting a lower frond (large leaf) and holding it down, gravity will cause the liquid to escape. In Madagascar, you can find the traveler's tree, with a cuplike sheath at the base of its leaves that collects water. In the western tropics of Africa, the leaf bases and roots of the umbrella tree can provide water. In the plains of northern Australia and Africa, the baobab tree collects water in its trunk during the wet season. These trees may contain clear, fresh water for weeks in dry weather.

Caution: Do not keep the sap from plants longer than 24 hours. It will begin to ferment, becoming unsafe to drink.

Water Stills

There are two main types of water stills: aboveground and belowground. Both can be used in almost any part of the world. Both work by drawing moisture either from the ground, plant material, or condensation. The disadvantage to the aboveground still is it can take up to 24 hours to get only 1 liter or quart of water. However, if you have the material at hand, more than one aboveground still can be constructed and other activities can be pursued while the stills are collecting water.

Aboveground Still

A clear plastic bag is required for making an aboveground still, and bigger is better. You'll need green leafy vegetation, but avoid poisonous plants. Poisonous plants will give you poisonous water. You'll also need a rock and a sunny slope to place your still. A straw or other suitable drinking tube will make this still more efficient.

1. Fill the plastic bag half to three-quarters of the way full with green leafy vegetation. Remove any sharp objects that may puncture the bag, like sticks or thorns.

2. Hold the bag's open end toward a breeze, or scoop in air to fill the bag. Place a small rock or a similar object into the bag.

3. Keeping as much air as possible in the bag, tie off the mouth of the bag as close to the end as possible. If you have a straw, reed, or piece of tubing, place it in the mouth of the bag before you tie it off.

4. Plug or tie off the end of your tubing so that air cannot escape.

5. Position the bag in direct sunlight on the slope with the mouth facing downhill. The bag should be settled with the rock at the low point of the bag.

6. Allow several hours for condensation to occur. Drink water from the still using the tube or reed, or loosen the tie around the bag's mouth so the water collected around the rock can be poured out.

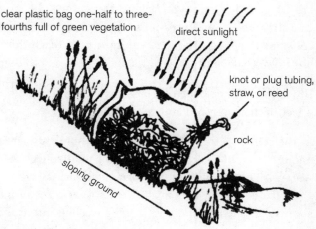

clear plastic bag one-half to three-fourths full of green vegetation

direct sunlight

knot or plug tubing, straw, or reed

rock

sloping ground

Aboveground still

7. Retie the bag and put it back into place for further condensation, or change out the old vegetation with new to provide maximum water output.

Belowground Still

The belowground still has the advantage of producing much more water than its counterpart, assuming you have a large enough plastic sheet and a digging tool. You'll also need a catch container, a drinking tube, and a rock.

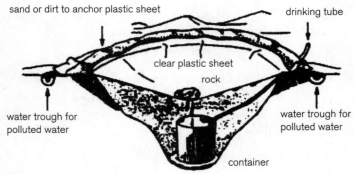

Belowground still

1. Find a location where you believe the soil may be moist. Dry streambeds or depressions where rainwater may have collected are good locations. Sunlight must reach this spot most of the day and the ground should be easy to dig.

2. Dig a hole in the shape of a large bowl. It should be 3 to 4 feet in diameter and about 2 feet deep.

3. In the center of this bowl, dig another hole only large enough to hold the container you'll use to collect the water. A container about the size of a quart jar works well. If a container isn't available, another piece of plastic slightly larger than the hole may be pushed into this hole by pleating the edges.

4. Anchor the tubing to the bottom of the container by forming a loose knot within the bowl but one that will still allow water to flow. Allow the other end of the tubing to reach out over the edge of the bowl.

5. Lay your plastic sheet loosely over the entire bowl-shaped hole and cover the edges with dirt to hold it in place. Your drinking tube should extend out past the bowl and beyond the edge of the plastic.

6. With a rock placed on the center of the plastic, slowly lower the plastic into the hole until it forms a cone shape. The apex of this cone should be 12 to 18 inches below the ground. Be sure that the rock is directly above the container and the plastic does not touch the wall of the large bowl. Completely cover the edges of the plastic.

7. Heat generated inside the large bowl, produced by the sun shining on the plastic, will cause moisture from the ground to evaporate. This evaporated moisture will condense on the underside of the plastic and drain back down toward the container. Using the tube, you can drink water from the container without disturbing the still. When not using, plug the end of the tube so moisture cannot escape.

You can collect more water by using available plants. To do this, you must increase the diameter of the larger bowl-shaped hole and allow room to place the plants around the inside of the bowl. Again, you must be careful that the plants do not touch the plastic.

If you have a source of polluted water, you can filter it using this still. Dig a trough about 1 foot away from the edge of the still. The trough needs to be about 1 foot deep and 3 inches wide. Pour the polluted water into the trough. The still will draw the polluted water from the trough through the soil. This water will then condense on the plastic and drain into the container. This system also works very well when salt water is your only source.

If the belowground still is your only source for water, you may need to construct at least three of these to have enough water to survive for any extended length of time. It takes at least three stills as described to meet individual daily water intake needs.

Water Purification

As I sat in my shelter or tended to other tasks while I waited for my bucket of snow to melt, the thought of "is this water safe" never crossed my mind. Rainwater and freshly fallen snow that has been melted in a clean container are both generally safe to drink. Growing up near and spending most of my time in the mountains, I often drank right out of a stream, river, or even one of the many lakes in central Oregon. However, I've always been careful to taste and look at the water and surrounding area. Sometimes I'd walk upstream a few hundred feet to test the air for bad smells, or look over the ground and water for dead fish, animals, or animal feces. I've also learned that a person's body will build immunities to some types of bacteria when constantly surrounded by them. People raised in the city and accustomed to drinking water that has always been sanitized before reaching their homes are more likely to have ill effects after drinking from the same streams or lakes that I have grown up with and drank from.

There have been times when the care I took may have saved me from becoming sick, or worse. Here in the higher elevations, streams and lakes are few and come from rain and snowmelt. Water is generally crystal clear in the mountains, but there are occasions when this is not so. An overflow of a river, stream, or lake may create areas of stagnant water. I avoid drinking from these and on occasion will stay well clear, simply because of the odor and mosquitoes they generate.

Rainwater is generally safe for anyone to drink. Water from plants is also usually safe to drink. However, unless you're sure of conditions and the source, purify water from lakes, ponds, streams, springs, and swamps, especially the water near human populations or in the tropics. When possible, always purify water you collect from vegetation or from the ground using iodine or chlorine, or by boiling.

When you're unsure if water is safe to drink, purification tablets are convenient and easy to use. Most businesses that cater to the hiker or backpacker will have them on hand. The cost is relatively inexpensive, they take up little room in a pack, and they come with instructions on use. Water can also be purified by placing five drops of 2 percent tincture of iodine in a full canteen of clear water. If the water is foggy, double the amount of iodine to 10 drops and let the canteen sit for 30 minutes before drinking. Boiling water for 1 minute at sea level and adding an additional minute for every thousand feet above sea level will also purify your water. If unsure of the elevation, boiling water for ten minutes will purify the water no matter where you are.

Many different methods and new products on the market will work well for water purification. Some of these products do have limitations on the parasites, bacteria, and other pathogens they kill or remove. Research the product you intend to use. My favorite standby is unscented household bleach. It takes only two to three drops in a canteen of water to disinfect. You may notice the taste of the bleach, but a small amount goes a long way. Be aware of expiration dates on any product you use.

When drinking water that has not been purified, you may be subjecting yourself to diseases or swallowing organisms that can harm you. Examples of some of these diseases include dysentery, cholera, flukes, giardia, and even leeches.

Water Filtration

Water filtration isn't the same as water purification. Water filtration only clears the water, making it more palatable, or easier to drink. If unsure of the safety of the water you're drinking, it must still be purified before drinking. There are two common ways to filter water: using a filtering device, or filling a container with water and letting it stand for 12 hours.

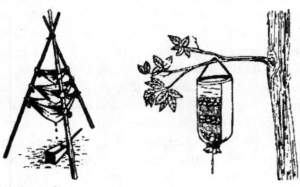

Examples of water filters

By allowing water to pass through a filtering device, such as a cloth or some other porous material, you remove only solid particles. I carry and have used household coffee filters to filter muddy water into a container for drinking on hikes. By adding layers of filtering material, such as sand or crushed rock, smaller particles of material can be removed from the water as it filters through your device. Adding crushed charcoal from a fire to your filter will give you an added advantage of removing bacteria from the water, but this method does not guarantee purification.

12

FIRE CRAFT

Remember Tom and Jerry from back in Chapter 8? They could have been better prepared for their survival adventure—certainly, they should have had a compass—but one item they did have, which ultimately saved their lives, was the means to build a fire.

When navigating the wilderness or any unfamiliar terrain, cold weather or spending a night in the outdoors generally requires the ability to start a fire. Fire can make the difference between living and dying. Fire can serve several purposes aside from providing warmth and comfort. A fire will cook and preserve your food, and this heated food will also provide warmth in the form of calories saved. Fire can also be used for signaling, purifying water, protecting against animals, and sterilizing bandages. If lost or on an extended journey, a fire will give you peace of mind and companionship, providing a psychological boost. You can also use fire to help in constructing tools and weapons.

Fire can also be the enemy when not treated with respect. Damaged equipment and even forest fires are generally the result of poor practice or lack of attention. Improper fire crafting skills can lead to severe burns. When used in shelters without precautions, fire can also lead to carbon monoxide poisoning and death.

Principles of Fire

To be proficient in fire craft, it helps to understand the basic principles of a fire. When you watch and observe a campfire, you may notice the wood itself does not burn directly. The flames are generated by the burning gas the wood produces as it's heated. It is the gas, combined with oxygen in the air, that burns.

To correctly construct a fire, it's important to understand the fire triangle. The three sides of the triangle represent air, heat, and fuel. All three are required to have a fire, and removing any one of the three will cause the fire to go out. Maximize a fire's potential by applying the proper ratio of these three elements. Like all navigation and survival skills, fire craft requires practice. To become proficient in building fires, practice your fire-making skills using different materials under a variety of adverse conditions.

Site Selection and Preparation

Before you build a fire, decide how you'll arrange the fire and on what site the fire will be placed. Several other things should be evaluated before building the fire, such as terrain and climate. Consider if there is enough nearby material available to build and maintain a fire, whether you have enough time and the tools to build the fire you need, and whether you need a fire for warmth, cooking, or some other purpose.

Before building your fire, you'll need a relatively dry spot that is protected from the wind. Secure the spot for your fire close to your shelter, if you have one. Make sure that the immediate area around the selected spot is clear. Remove brush, pine needles, or other objects, and scrape the soil to reduce any chance of fire spreading accidentally. To maximize the effectiveness of your fire, construct a firewall using rocks or logs (see page 102 for tips on building a fire-reflecting wall). This firewall will not only reflect and direct the heat to where it's needed; it will also protect you from the wind and cut down on flying sparks.

Caution: Avoid wet or porous rocks, as they may explode when heated.

Fire Material

There are three types of materials required to build a fire: tinder, kindling, and fuel. Tinder is any dry material that ignites with little heat. The tinder, when dry, will usually ignite with just a spark. Most preppers, survivalists, and outdoor enthusiasts alike are familiar with charred cloth, often referred to as char-cloth. Char-cloth holds a spark for long periods and is almost essential when you only have a ferro (ferrocerium) rod or similar device that only generates sparks. By placing a small amount of tinder on this spark, you can create a flame. Char-cloth is easily made by heating a cotton cloth until it turns black but does not catch fire. Prepare this cloth in advance and store it in an airtight container. A little bit goes a long way, and it takes up very little room in a survival kit. Other types of tinder could include birch bark, fine wood shavings, sawdust, needles, pocket lint, cotton, gunpowder, dead grasses, ferns, moss, or other dead and dry foliage.

Adding kindling to the ignited tinder to produce more heat is the second step to building a fire. Kindling should be completely dry and easy to ignite. When placed on the burning tinder, it should be small enough to ignite but large enough to create a bigger fire and more heat. Small twigs, branches, heavy cardboard, strips of wood, and split wood all make good kindling. A good fire made from kindling will be hot enough to burn the larger, less combustible material.

Use less combustible material that burns slowly and steadily as fuel for the fire. This material should only be added when the kindling is hot and burning well. Besides the large branches, dry standing branches, or fallen dry trees that are more commonly used as fuel, you can also use finely split green wood, dry grasses twisted into bunches, coal, oil shale, or dried animal dung.

How to Build a Fire

There are many ways to construct a fire, but this one stands alone in terms of its advantages. Unlike conventional fires that are normally built aboveground, the Dakota fire hole is built in the ground. This type of fire is generally smaller and is best suited for cooking food. It requires less fuel to maintain and works well in windy conditions. If you're lost and want a fire that can be seen from a distance or require a fire for warmth, then you should consider other options.

1. Dig a hole with a depth and diameter of 18 inches.

2. Find a spot 8 to 12 inches upwind of your first hole, then dig a hole with a diameter of 6 to 9 inches and a depth to match the fire hole.

3. Dig a tunnel between the bottoms of the two holes using a knife or twig.

4. Build the fire at the bottom of the larger hole.

The passageway between the two holes will allow air to flow down through the smaller hole to the bottom of the fire hole and feed the fire oxygen. The Dakota fire hole isn't limited in size, but the 18-inch hole described above works well. Practice building this type of fire. You may find that building one that is a little larger or even smaller will work better for you.

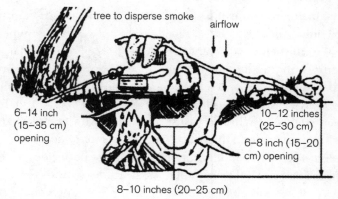

tree to disperse smoke

airflow

6–14 inch (15–35 cm) opening

10–12 inches (25–30 cm)

6–8 inch (15–20 cm) opening

8–10 inches (20–25 cm)

Dakota fire hole

Other Types of Fires

There are several common methods for building a fire, and they all have their own advantages. The conditions you find yourself in and the materials available will determine which fire is best. The fires listed further on can all be tweaked or modified to better fit your purpose. Practice building these fires under different conditions to increase your skill level. As explained in Chapter 9, remember to build a base for your fires or scrape away snow if you're building fire on saturated ground.

Tepee. When constructing a tepee fire, place sticks of kindling around the tinder in the shape of a tepee. Leave just enough room for you to ignite the tinder. I've found that placing a second layer of slightly

Tepee

larger pieces of kindling around the first will help. As the tepee burns, the outside sticks of wood will fall into the fire. This type of fire can work well even with wet wood.

Lean-to. This fire is built in the same manner as a lean-to shelter, only on a smaller scale. Unlike the shelter, you want the opening of this lean-to facing into the wind. At a 30-degree angle, insert into the ground a green stick that will not easily burn. Be sure the end of the stick is pointing into the wind. The tinder should be placed far under the stick. Lean kindling pieces against both sides of the lean-to stick and light the tinder. As the tinder spreads through the kindling, add more kindling or larger pieces of wood.

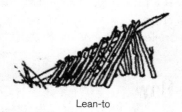
Lean-to

Cross-ditch. The cross-ditch is very simple but effective for encouraging airflow when starting a fire. Scratch or dig out a cross in the ground, about 12 inches in diameter and about 3 inches deep. Place your tinder in the center of the cross. Build a pyramid out of kindling above the tinder. The cross will allow oxygen to flow in under the pyramid. As the pyramid burns, add more kindling or larger pieces of wood.

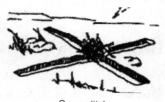
Cross-ditch

Pyramid. A pyramid fire is designed to burn downward. This type of fire burns slower and works well during the night, often requiring no attention. Lay this fire by placing two small logs on the ground,

Pyramid

12 to 18 inches apart. Place another layer of two logs across the top of the first two logs at a perpendicular angle. Add three or more layers of logs, each layer smaller than the previous one, at a perpendicular angle to the logs below. Make a starter fire on top of the pyramid you constructed. Keep the starter fire fueled until you see the logs just below it start to burn.

How to Light a Fire

Always light your fire from the upwind side, allowing any wind to push the flames farther into the fire. Lay your tinder, kindling, and fuel, or have these nearby before you ignite the fire. Take care in adding additional kindling and fuel as the fire begins to burn that you don't accidentally smother the fire completely.

To get the tinder burning requires heat, which is produced by igniters. These igniters fall under two categories: modern and primitive.

Modern Igniters

Modern igniters include those devices we normally think of as being used for fire starting, but others are not as commonly used. Some of these igniters have changed over the years, making the originals appear to be more primitive to some, but they are still considered modern. Almost anyone familiar with survival skills will carry conventional lighters for ease of use, but when the fuel runs out or when the lighters break, a reliable backup can save a lot of grief. The following are a few of the most popular ways to ignite a fire in an emergency, or when your regular lighter runs out of fuel, is damaged, or is lost.

Matches. Matches, commonly referred to as book or box matches, have been around longer than most other types of igniters and are still popular today. Book matches and some box matches generally require a strike pad to start burning. Some box matches are referred to as "strike anywhere matches" and are easily ignited by striking across any dry, rough surface. Matches are susceptible to moisture and require a waterproof container to protect them from any moisture.

Metal matches and ferro rods. Metal matches and ferro rods are available in a wide variety of shapes and sizes. They will generate sparks if they are struck or scraped with the appropriate tools. If you hold the matches or rod near the tinder and try to direct the sparks, some sparks will land on the tinder, causing it to smolder and eventually become a fire. These igniters have become quite popular among preppers, survivalists, and campers. My favorite is a metal matchbox. The metal box can be filled with a lighting fluid that will easily ignite the end of the metal match. With any igniter you decide to use, practice starting your fire. Use with different types of tinder under a variety of conditions to become proficient.

Convex lens. When you have nothing else to ignite a fire, a convex lens will do the trick. Unless you're already carrying around a magnifying glass, you may still have a lens if you have binoculars, telescopic sights, or eyeglasses. Hold the lens above the tinder at an appropriate angle to concentrate the sun's rays. Maintain this position until the tinder begins to smolder. Carefully place this smoldering tinder where needed. By gently blowing on or fanning the smoldering tinder, you can start a flame. Add small kindling and increase the pile in size as the fire begins to grow. With practice, the convex lens can guarantee you a fire, but only on bright, sunny days. It's also possible to ignite a fire by using a clear plastic bottle of water with a curved edge as your lens.

Primitive Igniters

When fire is needed in a real life emergency, primitive methods should be a last resort. If you're properly prepared, you will always have some modern means to ignite a fire. However, learning how to build a fire successfully using primitive methods is a skill that every adventurer should learn. There may be a time when you are without your modern lighter or it fails. Knowing how to ignite a fire using primitive methods will also give you a better understanding of how air, heat, and fuel work together in creating fire.

Some of my most gratifying moments as a prepper/survivalist included learning and becoming skilled at making a fire using only materials I could find. The feeling is much like what the actor Tom Hanks expressed in the movie *Cast Away* when he finally managed to create his first fire using a fire plow.

As the movie showed, a lot of practice and patience is required. Anyone can learn several techniques for building a primitive fire with a few sticks of wood. With a shoestring or similar object, you can take primitive to the high-tech level. The following techniques are based on friction and are the most commonly used primitive methods to create a fire.

Fire plow. The fire plow requires a base of softer wood and a shaft of harder wood. The base should be 12 to 18 inches long and a few inches wide, and should have a groove cut down the middle, about half the length of the wood.

hardwood

softwood

Fire plow

1. To start a fire, plow or rub the blunt tip of the harder wood shaft up and down the groove.

2. Small particles of wood will be pushed out of the end of the groove, creating a small pile of wood particles.

3. As you apply more pressure with each stroke, the heat generated by the friction will ignite the pile of wood particles.

Bow drill. The bow drill is simple to use in concept, but requires a lot of practice to master. It may take several attempts before you successfully create a fire, but don't give up. Once you have learned how to ignite a fire using a bow drill, other friction fire techniques will become easier to use. To use the bow drill method you'll need a socket, a drill, a fireboard, and a bow.

The socket is a stone, piece of hardwood, or bone that can easily be grasped in hand. It has to be concave or have a light depression on one side; it is used to hold the drill in place while applying downward pressure.

The drill needs to be a straight, hardwood stick about three quarters of an inch in diameter and 10 inches long. The top of the drill should be round and smooth to minimize friction against the socket. The bottom, or drill end, should be blunt to create more friction.

The base, or fireboard, may vary in size. A dry softwood board about 1 inch thick, 4 inches wide, and 12 to 18 inches long works well. Make or cut a depression about 1 inch inward from the 4-inch edge of your fireboard. Cut a V-shaped notch on this same edge of the board with the point of the V touching the depression.

The bow should be made from a green resilient stick about 3 feet long and about 1 inch in diameter. The type of wood isn't important. Without any slack, tie a bowstring (any piece of cordage) from one end of the bow to the other.

1. Have your fire materials ready before using the bow drill.

2. To use the bow drill, place your tinder under the V-shaped notch that was cut in the fireboard. I like to lay a flat piece of bark first, setting my tinder on top of the bark under the board. This allows me to easily pick up and work with my tinder once it's been ignited.

3. Once the tinder is in place, put one foot on the fireboard. Loop the bowstring over the drill and place the blunt end of the drill into the depression you created next to the V notch.

4. Hold the socket in one hand on top of the drill to hold the drill in place. Apply pressure on the drill while sawing back and forth to spin the drill.

5. As you work into a smooth motion, increase the pressure to the top of the drill while working the bow faster. The grinding action will cause embers to form and the tinder to smoke. Gently blow on the tinder until it ignites.

Bow and drill

Hand drill. The hand drill is another simple method, but a much harder one to master and use. It uses the same materials as the bow drill method, but without the bow, and requires a lot of energy, patience, and skill.

1. As with the bow drill, make a depression about 1 inch from the edge of your fireboard.

2. Cut a V-shaped notch on the edge of the board, with the point of the V touching the depression.

3. Place your tinder into the notch and the end of your drill onto the depression at the point of the notch.

4. With both hands at the top and on either side of the drill, rub your hands together while applying downward pressure. Repeat this process until embers form and the tender begins to smoke.

5. Gently blow on the tender to create a flame.

Two-man friction drill. The two-man friction drill works like the hand drill but requires less effort. One person applies downward pressure on the drill using a rock or another hard object with a concave surface or depression. The second person can rapidly rotate the drill by wrapping a length of cordage or shoestring around the middle of the drill and holding the ends in each hand.

SURVIVAL MEDICINE WHILE NAVIGATING

A navigator may face many problems, especially in rough terrain or extreme weather. The ability to treat medical problems that may arise is essential to reaching your destination safely.

No one is immune to accidents, sickness, or the effects of extreme weather. Without basic medical knowledge, success in the wilderness is put at risk. When traveling in a group, make sure one person has some basic medical skills before the trip begins.

This chapter will cover the basics of survival medicine, focusing on things you might encounter when land navigating, like requirements for maintaining health, water, food, and hygiene.[10] I will also cover some basics in handling bleeding, broken bones, wounds, and other common medical problems that may arise. For any serious prepper or survivalist, I would highly recommend taking a course in basic first aid and CPR. These courses can normally be found through your city directory or online. Having this basic knowledge may save a life, including your own, and will make you an asset in any group.

10 Amy and Joseph Alton, *The Survival Medicine Handbook*, (Doom and Bloom, 2013).

Water

Dehydration is one of the most common, yet often unrecognized, problems you might face when traveling in the wilderness. The average adult on an average day will lose half a gallon or more of water through sweating and other bodily functions. Exposure to hot or cold temperatures, high altitude, or physical activity will cause the body to lose even more water. In order to function properly and stay fit, lost water must be replaced.

The first signs of dehydration are often overlooked. Besides thirst, just a 5 percent loss of body fluids will lead to irritability, nausea, and weakness. A 10 percent loss will often be associated with dizziness, headaches, tingling in the arms and legs, and problems walking. At 15 percent, the loss of body fluid will result in dim vision, painful urination, swollen tongue, deafness, and a numbing of the skin. Losing 15 percent or more of your body fluids may lead to death.

Feeling tired even when you're not exerting yourself may be a symptom of dehydration. If you're feeling tired or fatigued, check for other common signs and symptoms associated with dehydration. By the time you crave fluids, you're already at least 2 percent dehydrated. Other symptoms of dehydration include dark urine with a strong order, low urine output, dark sunken eyes, mood swings, loss of skin elasticity, delayed capillary refill in fingernail beds when squeezed, trench line in the tongue, and thirst.

Pay attention to your heartbeat and your breathing, as these can also indicate your hydration level.[11]

- After losing 3 cups of body fluid, your pulse rate can reach 100 beats per minute with an increase of 10 to

11 Mayo Clinic Staff, "Dehydration," *Mayo Clinic*, Accessed Jan. 2017, http://www
.mayoclinic.org/diseases-conditions/dehydration/home/ovc-20261061.

20 breaths per minute. The usual breathing rate in an adult is 12 to 16 breaths per minute at rest.

- After losing 3 to 6 cups of fluid, your pulse rate will increase from 100 to 120 beats per minute and your breathing by 20 to 30 breaths per minute.

- After losing 6 to 8 cups of fluid, your pulse rate will increase from 120 to 140 beats per minute and your breathing by 30 to 40 breaths per minute.

When vital signs rise above these rates, advanced medical attention may be required.

Have water available at all times. Drink water regularly throughout the day, even if you're not thirsty, to replace the water you lose. Being thirsty isn't a sign of how much water you may actually need. Drink additional water when physically active, dealing with severe conditions, or under stressful situations. Lack of food can add to dehydration, so drink additional water to compensate for this low food intake. In severe climate conditions, especially hot, dry climates when fluid loss is at its greatest, the body may require up to three times the normal amount of fluids.

Loss of electrolytes (body salts) is associated with a heavy loss of water. There are several power drinks to provide these electrolytes; however, it's much simpler to carry a little salt in your pack. Adding a quarter teaspoon of salt to 4 cups of water will provide a concentration that the body can absorb.

In a survival situation, even when water is available, dehydration is quite common and the easiest thing to do is prevent it. The body uses water to help digest food. Always drink water while eating. Acclimation to adverse conditions will help the body perform more efficiently. Conserve sweat and ration water. Unless absolutely necessary, avoid those activities that may produce sweat. If low on water, ration what's available until you find a source. Severe dehydration can be prevented for up to a week or more with only two cups of sugar water (1 teaspoon of sugar per cup of water) each day, assuming activity is limited.

To estimate the loss of body fluids, keep in mind that a soaked T-shirt can hold 3 cups of fluid. A standard field bandage can hold 1 cup.

Food

Food provides the fuel your body burns to produce energy. While you can survive several weeks without food, mental and physical functions will slow quickly. To maintain good, active health, the body requires the vitamins, minerals, salts, and other elements found in food. As important to the physical health is the positive attitude, or morale, that food provides. The basic sources of food found in the wilderness include plants and animals, including fish. In different degrees, all provide the calories, carbohydrates, fats, and proteins the body requires to properly function.

Heat and potential energy are measured in calories. For the average person, 2,000 calories are needed daily to function at a minimum level. Starvation begins when the body's required caloric intake isn't provided.

Edible Plants

Plants can provide a main source of energy in the form of carbohydrates. Plants alone may not provide a balanced diet, but many plants like nuts and seeds will provide enough protein to keep the body at normal efficiency. Plants like roots and vegetables contain natural sugars that will provide calories and carbohydrates.

Plants can be carried more easily than meat and can be made to last longer by drying in the wind, air, sun, or fire. Knowledge of plants becomes more important in areas where meat is scarce. There are many books available where you can learn about the different edible plants and where they grow.

Animals as Food

Animal meat may be more abundant than edible plants in some areas, and it is a better source for nutrients. However, you need some different skill sets to get meat. In a survival situation when food is an immediate priority, look for wildlife that is easier to obtain. Insects, crustaceans, fish, and reptiles may be easier to catch and satisfy any immediate need while you're preparing traps or snares for larger animals.

Hygiene

We may become our own worst enemies when navigating the wilderness without personal hygiene. Hygiene is the first step in keeping infections and disease at bay and increasing chances of survival. In most situations, a routine shower with hot water and soap is only a pleasant thought. Instead, you're cleaning yourself with a rag and soapy water. Nevertheless, it's important to keep yourself clean and pay special attention to your feet, armpits, crotch, hands, and hair, as these areas are susceptible to infection and infestation. If water is unavailable, an air bath is better than no bath. Simply remove as much clothing as possible to expose the skin to the sun and air for at least one hour. If you don't have soap, use ashes or sand, or make soap from animal fat and wood ashes if your situation allows.

Bodily hygiene. Hopefully you have soap, but even without it, it's important to stay as clean as possible using any means available. Special consideration should be given to your hands. Hands that are not clean are prone to pass germs onto anything they touch, especially food or wounds. Always wash your hands after handling any items that may carry germs and before handling food, food utensils, or drinking water. Keep fingernails clean and trimmed. Keep your hair clean to protect against bacteria and to help prevent fleas, lice, and other parasites. Keeping your hair short, combed, and trimmed will help you avoid these dangers.

Oral hygiene. Poor oral hygiene can make any good day a bad day and a bad day worse. Keep your mouth and teeth clean by using a toothbrush at least once a day. If a toothbrush isn't available, make one. Chew the end of a twig or small stick to separate the fibers, then use it as a toothbrush. A strip of cloth wrapped around your finger can also be used to help keep your teeth clean. If toothpaste isn't available, use baking soda, soap, salt, or small amounts of fine sand to brush with. After brushing, rinse your mouth with salt water, willow bark tea, or warm plain water if nothing else is available. Flossing your teeth with string or strands from cordage will also help in oral hygiene. Cavities can be temporarily filled after cleaning using candle wax, aspirin, tobacco, toothpaste, or ginger root.

Clothing and bedding. To reduce the chances of skin infection and parasitic infestation, clothing and bedding must be kept clean. Wear clean undergarments and socks daily. When water is a problem, air-clean your clothing and bedding by shaking them out or brushing them off and allowing them to air out in the sun for at least two hours. If using a sleeping bag, turn it inside out and allow it to air.

Campsite hygiene. Keep your camp area clean by not soiling it with urine or feces. For waste, dig a hole away from and downwind of your camp. Keep your waste hole away from your food and water supply. Cover the waste hole after each use.

Rest. Rest is important for maintaining morale. Plan regular rest breaks throughout the day. Learn to make yourself comfortable when conditions are poor. Break up the routine. When conditions do not permit total relaxation, change from physical to mental activities and back again when possible. This can be refreshing and good for morale.

Foot Care

Feet, don't fail me now! Having serious foot problems can lead to disaster in the wilderness. Without proper care, serious conditions can leave you immobile and make survival a challenge, if not impossible. Take precautionary steps before planning a trip into the wilderness. Wear only the proper shoes for the terrain you'll be navigating. Break in your shoes and know they will be comfortable before heading out into the wilderness. Wear the right-sized dry socks and insoles, if needed.

Blisters are the most common source of foot aggravation, and if not treated properly, they can lead to infections that are more serious. An unopened blister is safe from infection. If you have a small blister, relieve the pressure and reduce any friction by adding a padding material around the blister. If a blister pops or opens up, treat the blister as if it were an open wound. Clean and dress it as often as needed and pad around it.

If a large blister looks prone to popping or tearing, there are steps that can be taken to help eliminate any problems and get you back on your way. If you have a clean sewing needle and clean thread, run the needle and thread through the blister, leaving both ends of the thread hanging outside the blister. The thread will absorb the liquid inside. This will reduce the size of the hole and ensure the hole will not close up, allowing the blister to dry and heal quickly. If a needle and thread are not available, use a clean pointed object to pierce the blister along an edge. Carefully squeeze out the fluid by rolling your thumb or finger toward the hole you made from the opposite side of the blister. This procedure may take several attempts as the blister continues to fill with fluid. Once all the fluid has been removed, add padding around the blister.

HOW TO MAKE SOAP

1. Extract grease from animal fat by cutting the fat into small pieces and cooking it in a pot.

2. While cooking the fat, add enough water to the pot to keep the fat from sticking. Continue to cook the fat slowly, stirring frequently.

3. After the fat is rendered, pour the grease into a container to harden.

4. While waiting for the grease to harden, place ashes in a container with a spout near the bottom. Pour water over the ashes and collect the liquid that drips out of the spout in a separate container. This liquid is the potash, or lye. Another way to get the lye is to pour the slurry (the mixture of ashes and water) through a straining cloth.

5. In a cooking pot, mix two parts grease to one part potash and place this mixture over a fire to boil until it thickens.

6. After the mixture cools, it will be safe as soap. You can use it in the semiliquid state directly from the pot. You can also pour it into a pan, allow it to harden, and cut it into bars for later use.

Medical Emergencies

Fortunately, most medical problems that may arise in the wilderness are not serious, but often they will require some sort of treatment. The experienced adventurer is prepared to deal with these problems and has the knowledge to overcome other serious medical emergencies as well. Medical emergencies that you should consider and prepare for include breathing problems, severe bleeding, shock, and all of the other situations discussed in this chapter.

Before any action can be taken in a medical emergency, a quick physical exam must be performed to isolate the problem. Look for the cause of the injury, starting with the airway and breathing tubes, unless severe bleeding is noticeable. In some cases, a person may die more quickly from severe bleeding than suffocation.

Breathing Problems

There are a number of reasons breathing problems may occur. The most common cause is airway obstruction, which may occur due to foreign matter in the mouth or throat. Face and neck injuries, or a kink in the throat when the neck is bent forward, may also block the passage of air. Breathing can also be slowed or stopped because of swelling and inflammation caused by allergic reactions or the inhalation of smoke, flames, or irritating vapors. If a person is unconscious, the muscles in the lower jaw and tongue relax as the neck drops forward, causing the tongue to fall back and block the airway.

To restore breathing, you can attempt CPR. *Caution:* CPR and many other medical treatments explained within this book should not be attempted unless by an individual trained in the procedure or when no other options are available.

Check the victim for airway obstruction. If the person can cough or speak, let the person try to clear the obstruction naturally. Watch the victim and be ready to clear the airway and perform mouth-to-mouth resuscitation, should the person become unconscious. If the airway is completely blocked, administer abdominal thrusts, also called the Heimlich maneuver, until the obstruction is cleared, and then perform CPR.

When performing CPR, use your finger to clear the mouth of any foreign matter or objects, dirt, broken teeth, or dentures. Grasp the angles of the victim's entire lower jaw and lift with both hands, one on each side, moving the jaw forward. For stability, rest your elbows on the surface on which the victim is lying. If his lips are closed, open the lower lip with your thumb.

With the victim's airway open, pinch the nose closed with thumb and finger and blow two complete breaths into the lungs. Let the lungs deflate and watch for the chest to rise and fall while listening for air during exhalation. With your  cheek near the victim's mouth, feel for this flow of air. If breathing does not begin on its own, continue performing mouth-to-mouth resuscitation.

Bleeding

In a survival situation, severe bleeding must be controlled immediately. A person can die within a matter of minutes when lost blood cannot be replaced. External bleeding can be controlled by direct pressure, indirect pressure (pressure points), or a tourniquet.

Direct pressure. The most common and effective way to control bleeding is with direct pressure. Direct pressure must be applied firmly over a wound for a long enough time to stop the bleeding. If the bleeding continues after 30 minutes, apply a pressure dressing. A pressure dressing should consist of thick gauze or other suitable material applied directly over the wound and held in place with a tightly wrapped bandage. This bandage should be loose enough to allow the flow of blood but tighter than a normal bandage. Once the bandage is applied, do not remove it even if it becomes blood soaked. Leave the pressure bandage in place for one or two days before replacing it with a smaller bandage. After this point, replace the bandage daily and watch for signs of infection.

By elevating a bleeding injury over the heart, you can slow blood loss and potentially relieve pain, but elevation alone will not control bleeding; direct pressure must also be applied.

Pressure points. Pressure points are main arteries that can be found near the surface of the skin. Normally there is more than one artery supplying blood to the veins, but applying direct pressure to an artery may help to slow the bleeding until a pressure bandage is applied.

Pressure points are located in the underside of the arms, crook of elbows, front of wrists and ankles, underside of knees, midway of groin, above the clavicle, side of jaw, and in the temple. If you cannot remember the exact location of pressure points, apply pressure to the joint just above the injured area.

Tourniquet. A tourniquet should only be used when no other method can control the bleeding. A tourniquet left in place for too long can cause tissue damage, which could lead to gangrene followed by the loss of the limb. A tourniquet not applied properly may also cause damage to nerves and other areas near the site.

If a tourniquet must be used, place it around the limb, between the wound and the heart, 2 to 4 inches away from the wound. Never place the tourniquet directly over the wound or a fractured bone. Use a stick or other suitable object as a handle to tighten the tourniquet, and only tighten enough to stop the flow of blood. Secure the tourniquet by tying one end to the limb. If alone, never release or remove the tourniquet. However, a companion can release the pressure every 10 to 15 minutes for 1 to 2 minutes to allow the blood to flow to the rest of the extremity and prevent limb loss.

Shock

The possibility of shock should be considered with all injuries. If the injured person is conscious, place him on a level surface and elevate the legs 6 to 12 inches. If the victim is unconscious, place her on her side or abdomen with the head turned to one side to prevent choking on blood or vomit and to allow breathing. If you're unsure of the best position, place him perfectly flat and do not move him.

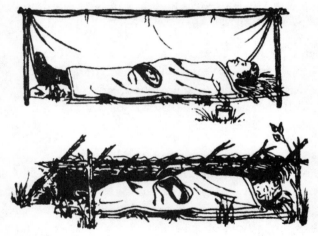

Treating shock

Keep an injured person as warm as possible. Change out any wet clothing with dry clothes, if possible, and improvise a shelter for protection from the weather. Build a fire or small fires around the victim for warmth. Provide external warmth by placing canteens with heated water, or heated rocks wrapped in clothing, around the victim. You can also lie next to the victim to transfer body heat. If the injured person is awake, offer small amounts of warmed liquids, including salt or sugar solutions if they are available. If you're alone, find protection from the weather and rest lying down, with your head lower than your feet.

Bone Fractures and Joint Injury

Navigating through rough terrain can lead to accidents. Fractures, sprains, or dislocated joints are the most common injuries that you might experience in the wilderness. Navigation may still be possible depending on the severity of these injuries, but most will only get worse and may leave you stranded if some type of treatment is not provided.

Fractures may either be open or closed, with the open (compound) fracture generally being much more serious. With the compound fracture, the exposed end of the broken bone breaks through the skin to create an open wound. After setting the bone, the wound must be treated as any other open wound. The closed fracture has no open wound, but both open and closed fractures will generally require a splint to make further travel possible and reduce pain.

A closed fracture can be harder to identify but will show signs. Some of the signs to look for include:

- pain

- tenderness

- discoloration

- swelling

- loss of use

- a grating sound when the broken ends of bone rub together

With a fracture, the affected limb must be immobilized to reduce the possibility of any further damage. Internal bleeding may already be occurring due to severed vessels at the injury. If the area below the break shows signs of numbness, swelling, coolness, or paleness, and you see signs of shock, a major vessel may have been cut. The bleeding must be controlled and lost fluids replaced while the injured person rests.

Often, traction to the fractured limb must be maintained while applying a splint. Arms and other smaller bones can be pulled into place by hand. For an arm or leg fracture, the V-notch of a tree may work for traction by placing the wrist of the broken arm or ankle of the broken leg into the V and pushing against the tree with the other limb. Once the broken limb is pulled back into place you can then splint the break.

A broken femur (thighbone) may be much more difficult to maintain traction because of the stronger leg muscles. In this case, when professional help is not available, a traction splint may be used. The cross member on the bottom of the splint will maintain the traction while the upper portion of the body and splint carries the body weight.

Dislocations. Dislocations, the separation of bone joints, can be extremely painful and hinder progress in wilderness travel. Depending on the degree, they can also cause issues with nerve and circulatory functions. Joints must be placed back into alignment as soon as possible. Dislocations can normally be identified by

- joint pain

- tenderness

- swelling

- discoloration

- deformity

- loss of joint mobility

In the field, the easiest and safest way to treat a dislocation is by manual traction or by using weights to set the joints back into their proper place. When the realignment is done, the pain will ease and a more normal use of the joint will be evident. You can judge proper alignment by the look and feel of the joint and by comparing it to the same joint on the opposite side of the body.

Once the joint has been realigned, immobilize the joint using a splint. Splint the area with padding for comfort above and below the joint. Check that circulation continues after splinting the joint. Remove the splints after 7 to 14 days and gradually use the injured joint until healed.

Sprains. Sprains are quite common when traveling rough terrain, causing pain, swelling, tenderness, and discoloration. While navigation may still be possible, care must be given to reduce as much workload as possible on the affected area. In ideal situations, it is best to treat a sprain by resting the injured area. If possible, apply ice to the injured area for several hours, then switch to heat after that. Use wrapping and/or splinting to keep the area immobile. If it's an ankle or other foot sprain, leave the boot on unless it creates a problem with circulation. Elevating the affected area will also help in healing and ease the pain.

Wounds

For the prepper and survivalist, wounds can come in many different forms, all of which are characterized by issues affecting the skin.

The most common are open wounds. If these are not treated, they can become serious threats to a survival situation. Besides the tissue damage associated with open wounds, there will likely be blood loss and infection. Infection can be caused by any bacteria transferred from the cause of the wound, clothing being worn, or other foreign matter that encounters the wound. When possible, the first step taken to treating an open wound is to clean the wound as soon as possible to prevent further contamination.

Remove or cut away any clothing that may come into contact with the wound. If a sharp object, gunshot, or other object caused the wound, be sure to look for signs of an exit wound. Clean the entire area around the wound and rinse with generous amounts of water. If water isn't available, use fresh urine.

Unless conditions dictate, do not suture the wound; instead, use the "open treatment" method. While an open wound may look bad or even smell, leaving it open will allow any pus caused by infection to drain. Cover the wound with a clean dressing and hold the dressing in place with a bandage. Check the wound daily for infection and change the dressing. If the wound is gaping, hold the edges together using pieces of adhesive tape cut in the shape of a butterfly or dumbbell.

When inflicted with a wound during a survival situation, there will almost always be infection. Common signs of infection include pain, swelling, redness around the wound, high temperatures, and pus on the wound and dressing. If not treated, infection may get worse, leading to more difficult problems or even death.

When infection is evident, treat it by placing a warm, moist compress directly on the infected area. Keep the warm compress on the wound for 30 minutes or until the compress cools. Drain the wound, dress, and bandage. Drink lots of water. Repeat this process three or four times a day until all signs of the infection are gone.

If a wound becomes severely infected and no antibiotics are available, an ancient method still practiced today may be the answer: maggot debridement, or maggot therapy.[12]

Under survival conditions, expose the wound to flies, and then cover the wound. Check the wound daily for maggots. When you notice them, keep the wound covered, and keep checking daily. The maggots will eat away all the dead tissue before they start eating the healthy tissue. When you notice increased pain and bright red blood, the maggots have reached healthy tissue. Rinse the wound with sterile water or fresh urine to remove all the maggots. Check the wound every four hours for several days to make sure all maggots have been removed, then bandage and treat as any other wound.[13]

Bites and Stings

Not only are they irritating, but insects and other pests can be a hazard in a survival situation. Ticks, mosquitoes, flies, fleas, and lice are just a few of the many that can bring on diseases and allergic reactions in some people. The best way to avoid potential problems is to keep immunization shots up to date, wear clothing that will help cover all exposed skin, use netting and insect repellent, and when possible, avoid insect-infested areas.

When bitten or stung, do not scratch the area, as this may lead to infection. Be mindful of your body: Inspect at least once a day for bites, and ensure there are no insects or ticks attached to you. If you find ticks attached to your skin, do not try to pull them off. Instead, cover the tick with a petroleum-based product such as motor oil or Vaseline. You can also use tree

12 Carrie Arnold, "New Science Shows How Maggots Heal Wounds," *Scientific American*, April 1, 2013, Accessed Jan. 2017, https://www.scientificamerican.com/article/news-science-shows-how-maggots-heal-wounds.

13 Gwendolyn Cazander, et al, "Synergism between Maggot Excretions and Antibiotics," *Wound Repair and Regeneration* 18, no. 6 (2010) 637-642, http://onlinelibrary.wiley.com/doi/10.1111/j.1524-475X.2010.00625.x/abstract.

sap. This will cut off their air supply and force them to release their hold.

The list of possible bites and stings is too long to cover all the different potential treatments. However, almost all can be treated in the same manner if in a survival situation.

Immunizations are important to prevent common diseases, including many carried by mosquitoes and other insects. Consider finding out what infectious diseases are seen where you travel. Antibiotics will treat bacterial disease. Some of the more useful are in the Penicillin, Erythromycin, and Tetracycline families. Have some available and be familiar with their use, but realize that there is an epidemic of antibiotic resistance; they should be employed rarely and with caution.

Bee and wasp stings. If stung by a bee, immediately remove the stinger by scraping with a knife or fingernail. Never remove the stinger with your fingers; this may force more venom into the wound. Wash the area with soap and water to reduce infection. Your pack should contain a medical kit, which should include a sting kit if you're susceptible to allergic reactions caused by stings. You can relieve the irritation caused by stings and insect bites by using a cold compress or covering the area with mud, ashes, crushed cloves of garlic, or onion.

Spider bites and scorpion stings. The most common spider bites to be concerned about are those from the black widow, known by the red hourglass on its abdomen, and the funnel-web spider found in Australia. The symptoms and treatment for both are the same. Pain isn't severe immediately after a bite, but it soon develops at the site of the bite, then spreads over the entire body, eventually settling in the abdomen and legs. Cramps and nausea, along with vomiting, are common, and a rash may occur. Tremors, sweating, and salivation may also occur, along with anaphylactic reactions. These symptoms will start to fade after a few hours and will disappear in a few days.

The brown recluse spider, sometime referred to as the fiddleback spider for the violin shape on its back, will cause little or no pain when it bites. However, after a few hours, a painful red area with a blue or purple center will appear. A week or two after the initial bite, the area will turn dark and mummified. The scab will fall off, leaving an open ulcer that does not heal. Reactions that will follow and may lead to death include fever, chills, joint pain, vomiting, and rash.

First aid treatment. The funnel-web spider bite requires pressure, immobilization, bandaging, and splinting of the bitten limb that may delay venom spread. With black widow and brown recluse spider bites, use an ice-pack. Keep the patient calm and seek medical attention. If possible, take the spider (dead or alive) to the hospital for identification.

Large hairy spiders, known as tarantulas, are mainly found in the tropics. Most tarantulas do not inject venom, but some South American species do. They have large fangs, and if bitten, the bite will be painful and bleed. Treat a tarantula bite as an open wound (see page 151). If signs of poisoning appear, treat in the same manner as a black widow spider bite.

Scorpions are all poisonous to some degree, and their bites can cause two different reactions, depending on the species. Some scorpion bites will only cause a reaction around the sting. This may include swelling around the area, a prickly sensation around the mouth, and a thick feeling of the tongue. Severe reactions include respiratory difficulties, body spasms, drooling, gastric distention, double vision, blindness, involuntary rapid movement of the eyeballs, involuntary urination and defecation, and heart failure. Death is rare, occurring mainly in children and adults with high blood pressure or illnesses. Treat scorpion stings as you would treat black widow bites.

Snakebites. Unless the snake feels antagonized, the odds of getting a snakebite in a survival situation are small. The possibility remains, however, and you should know how to treat a snakebite. Snakebites can affect morale, and though more than half of those who get snakebites suffer little or no poisoning, and only about one quarter of those bitten develop serious systemic poisoning, not knowing how to treat snakebites properly can result in tragedy.

Along with bacteria, the digestive enzymes that aid snakes in digesting their food can be left at the site of the bite. The bacteria can lead to infection, while the enzymes destroy tissue to leave a large, open wound. If left untreated, this condition could lead to amputation. Snake venom also contains poisons, specifically neurotoxins, that attack the victim's central nervous system and blood circulation. Symptoms of a poisonous bite may be spontaneous bleeding from the nose and anus, blood in the urine, pain at the site of the bite, and swelling at the site of the bite. These symptoms may occur within a few minutes or up to two hours later. Breathing difficulty, paralysis, weakness, twitching, and numbness are also signs of neurotoxic venoms. These signs usually appear 1.5 to 2 hours after the bite.

If you determine that an individual has been bitten by a poisonous snake, reassure the victim and keep him still. Clean the bite area and remove any constricting items such as watches, rings, and bracelets. Keep the victim's airway clear and be ready to preform mouth-to-mouth resuscitation or CPR. Immobilize the area and use a constricting band or tourniquet between the wound and the heart.

Do not give the victim alcohol, tobacco products, or depressants. Do not make any deep cuts at the bite site. This could create a direct route into the bloodstream for venom and infection.

Note: If medical treatment is over one hour away, make an incision over each puncture—no longer than $\frac{1}{4}$-inch (6 mm) and no deeper than $\frac{1}{8}$-inch (3 mm)—cutting just deep enough to enlarge the fang opening, but only through the first or second layer of skin. Place a suction cup over the bite so that you have a good vacuum seal. Suction the bite site three or four times. Use mouth suction only as a last resort, and only if you do not have open sores in your mouth. Spit the envenomed blood out and rinse your mouth with water. This method will draw out 25 to 30 percent of the venom.

If there are signs of infection, keep the wound open and clean. Keep the wound covered with dry, sterile dressing. Have the victim drink large amounts of fluids until the infection is gone.

EPILOGUE:
Start Your Own Adventure

When I was first approached to write this book, I thought, "What a great idea!" It was an adventure in itself to put what I know about land navigation into words and share my experience. I soon found it to be a daunting task, as I was not comfortable putting anything on paper without first confirming my information through many other resources. I found, as with any new adventure, there is always something new to learn.

Whether you are a prepper, survivalist, or an outdoor enthusiast, there is always something new and exciting to be found around the next corner. While this book is intended to help you find your way there and back again, know that landscape navigation also requires patience, practice, and the right tools. If you do not own a compass or a map, you are missing the tools needed to optimize this book.

Keep your book, map, and compass handy, and practice the techniques taught within by yourself or with family and friends. In any situation, you will know where you're going with confidence, and you can be the "go-to" person in your group when camping out in areas you may not have considered before or when in a survival situation.

REFERENCES

Alton, Amy and Joseph. *The Survival Medicine Handbook*. Doom and Bloom, 2013.

Gooley, Tristan. *The Natural Navigator*. www.thenatural navigator.com.

Headquarters, Department of the Army. "FM 21-76. *US Army Survival Manual*," US Army. June 1999. Accessed Jan. 2017.

Headquarters, Department of the Army. "FM 3-25.26. *Map Reading and Land Navigation*," US Army. January 2005, Accessed Jan. 2017.

Martin, Walter Glen. *Prepper Broadcasting Network*. www.prepperbroadcasting.com.

McCullough, Jay, ed. *The Complete US Army Survival Guide to Tropical, Desert, Cold Weather, Mountain Terrain, Sea, and NBC Environment*. Skyhorse, 2016.

INDEX

T

U

ACKNOWLEDGMENTS

To Shayna of Ulysses Press, Jean, Pappy, Highlander, Wolfe, James, Cat, and Linda, as well as all the others that visit in the chat room or are associated in other ways with Prepper Broadcasting. With special regards to my two sons Tom and Logan. Thanks for your help and support in making this book possible.

ABOUT THE AUTHOR

Born in California, **Walter "Glen" Martin** was raised at the base of the Strawberry Mountains and later near the Cascade Mountains of Oregon. He spent his youth as an avid hunter and fisherman. Knowing how to live off the land, it was not uncommon for Glen to head up into the mountains on a hunting or fishing trip with little more than his rifle or fishing pole.

After earning his degrees in architecture and mechanical drafting, Glen spent the next 30 years as a design consultant in several Western states, including Alaska. Now living in the mountains of northern Idaho with his fiancé, Glen has settled into an off-grid lifestyle. He owns and operates Prepper Broadcasting, a 24/7 Internet radio station devoted to self-reliance and independence. When not at his desk, you're likely to find Glen somewhere in the mountains.